Religion in America

·ADVISORY EDITOR

Edwin S. Gaustad

TO WIN THE WEST

Missionary Viewpoints
1814-1815

ARNO PRESS

A NEW YORK TIMES COMPANY

New York • 1972

Reprint Edition 1972 by Arno Press Inc.

Report of a Missionary Tour Through That Part of the
United States Which Lies West of the Allegany Mountains
was reprinted from a copy in The Union Theological
Seminary Library
Report to the Secretary of the Society for Propagating
the Gospel Among the Indians [1814] was reprinted from
a copy in The University of Illinois Library

RELIGION IN AMERICA - Series II
ISBN for complete set: 0-405-04050-4
See last pages of this volume for titles.

Manufactured in the United States of America

Publisher's Note: The selections in this compilation
were reprinted from the best available copies.

Library of Congress Cataloging in Publication Data
Main entry under title:

To win the West.

    (Religion in America, series II)
    Reprint of A correct view of that part of the United
States which lies west of the Allegany Mountains, with
respect to religion and morals, by J. F. Schermerhorn
and S. J. Mills, first published 1814; of Report of a
missionary tour through that part of the United States
which lies west of the Allegany Mountains, by S. J.
Mills and D. Smith, first published 1815; and of Report
...respecting the Indians inhabiting the western parts
of the United States, by J. F. Schermerhorn, first published 1814.

    1. Mississippi Valley--Church history. 2. Missis-
sippi Valley--Description and travel. 3. Missions
--Mississippi Valley. 4. Indians of North America
--Mississippi Valley. I. Schermerhorn, John Freeman.
A correct view of that part of the United States which
lies west of the Allegany Mountains. 1972. II. Mills
Samuel John. Report of a missionary tour through that
part of the United States which lies west of the
Allegany Mountains. 1972. III. Schermerhorn, John
Freeman. Report...respecting the Indians inhabiting
the western parts of the United States. 1972.
BR540.T6 1972   266'.022   73-38467
ISBN 0-405-04091-1

Contents

A

CORRECT VIEW

OF

THAT PART OF THE UNITED STATES

WHICH LIES WEST OF THE

ALLEGANY MOUNTAINS,

WITH REGARD TO RELIGION AND MORALS.

BY JOHN F. SCHERMERHORN,
AND
SAMUEL J. MILLS.

HARTFORD :

PETER B. GLEASON AND CO. PRINTERS.
....
1814.

ADVERTISEMENT.

In the summer of 1812, Messrs. John F. Schermerhorn and Samuel J. Mills commenced a tour through the western and southern parts of the United States, under the patronage of the Massachusetts Missionary Society, and the Missionary Society of Connecticut. They were instructed not only to perform missionary services, but to enquire particularly into the religious and moral state of that part of the country. They completed the tour in about one year. The result of their enquiries, as communicated to the Trustees of the Missionary Society of Connecticut, is now submitted to the public, by direction of said Trustees.

MR. SCHERMERHORN'S STATEMENT.

TO THE TRUSTEES OF THE MISSIONARY SOCIETY OF CONNECTICUT;

GENTLEMEN,

THE report which I have at this time the pleasure of transmitting to you, will probably be found to differ from the ordinary mode on such occasions. I have omitted to give you the transactions of each day in detail, because the information I have to communicate, thus presented, it would be impossible for any other person so to arrange, as to give the Society a just conception of the state of the churches, religion, and morals in the States and Territories west of the Allegany Mountains.

A correct view of the state of religious affairs, in that region, is of the utmost importance ; for the knowledge which this part of the country at present possesses, on this subject, is very limited and partial. Unless a proper representation of the case be made, we have no reason to expect that Christians will feel the necessity of contributing with that liberality, which will enable Missionary Societies to support missionaries in the western country ; nor ministers of the Gospel feel it their duty, personally to engage in them. These reasons are my apology for departing from the ordinary mode of communication. As it respects my labors as a missionary, besides the services of the Sabbath. I preached during the week, as frequently as the people could be convened, and other circumstances would admit. Some weeks three times, other weeks not more than once or twice ; and it has happened also, that I have had no service except on the Sabbath

Every State has its natural as well as civil divisions. The situation of the civil, such as counties and townships, it is not expected will be known by persons residing out of the State ; while its natural divisions are known by all who are conversant with Geography. It is proposed, therefore, to take natural divisions of the country, and show in Statistical Tables, the counties they comprehend, and the inhabitants, ministers, churches, and vacancies, among the different denominations in the same; accompanied with such remarks as may occur.

The denominations generally noticed in the Tables are Presbyterians, Baptists, and Methodists. The Congregationalists, Associate Reformed Church, Associate Synod, Covenanters, and those churches in connection with the " General Assembly of the Presbyterian Church in the United States," are all classed under the title of Presbyterians; for those minor considerations, concerning the externals of religion, which now separate them, and which originated in causes generally not existing in this country, do not appear of sufficient consequence, in a missionary point of view, to merit separate notice.

PENNSYLVANIA WEST OF THE ALLEGANY MOUNTAINS.

The District of Country situated between the Allegany Mountain and River, extending South from Kiskemanetas River, to the New York State line, comprises the following

Counties.	Inhab.	Presbyterians.			Methodists.	
		Min.	Ch. Sup.	Vac. So.	Preac.	Mem.
Warren,	827					
M'Keen,	142					
Potter,	29					
Tioga,	1,687					
Venango,	3,060	....	....	....	2	486
Jefferson,	161					
Clearfield,	875					
Cambria,	2,117					
Indiana,	6,214	1	2	2		
Armstrong,	6,143	2	4	1		
Total,	21,255	3	6	3	2	486

The land is very broken and mountainous, with a light and comparatively poor soil, and will not probably settle with any great degree of rapidity. In the ten counties, which this district comprises, is a population of only 21,255 souls, which must, necessarily, be very scattered. There are only 3 Ministers, 6 churches supplied with preaching part of the time, and 3 vacant societies of the Presbyterian order. Of the Baptists in Pennsylvania, I was not able to procure any particular account. The Methodists have one entire circuit in this district, and probably parts of others.

Eight of these counties, it will be perceived, are entirely destitute of preachers, unless they are occasionally visited by an itinerant Methodist. I apprehend that nothing can be done here towards forming societies, because the people generally are indigent. The General Assembly have sent missionaries into this part of the country, occasionally, for a few weeks. But it is to be feared that such transient missions, among the rude and ignorant, are of very little utility They need constant instruction, and to the regular routine of the Methodists' visits monthly must be attributed their success, in the western country, while our missions frequently end without building up one Society.

The District between the Allegany Mountains and the Allegany and Ohio Rivers ; and between Conemaugh River on the north, and the Virginia State line on the south, comprises the following

Counties.	Inhab-itants.	Presbyterians.			Methodists.		Other De-nominations.
		Min.	Ch.sup	Vac soc	Itine-rants.	Mem-bers.	
Somerset,	11,284	..	...	4	..	...	Ger. Presb.
Fayette,	24,714	3	6	3	2	650	do.
Greene,	12,544	1	...	2	2	573	
Washington,	36,289	13	20	1	..	...	Some Bap.
Westmoreland,	26,392	9	16	10	2	880	do.
Allegany	25,317	10	21	1	1	177	Some Cath.
Total,	136,540	36	63	21	7	2,280	

It appears that these six counties have a population of 136,540, 36 ministers, 63 churches supplied by them with preaching, and 21 vacant societies, all of the Presbyterian order. It is evident from this, that most of the preachers have to supply two or three societies. This district is not in very pressing need of missionary assistance, compared with other parts of the country, except it be the counties of Somerset and Greene, which have a population of nearly 24,000 inhabitants, and not one church supplied with preaching.

There are a few German societies in Somerset, Fayette, and Westmoreland. The Methodists have seven itinerants in this district, and 2280 members belonging to their society. In Allegany county, at Pittsburg, there is an Episcopalian church, the only one in the west part of the State. There are also a few Halcyons on ten mile river, in Washington county, but in general there are fewer sectaries* here than in any other part of the western country. The public, and men of information and influence, are decidedly in favor of Presbyterianism.

* The word Sectaries is used merely as a term of distinction, to denote all religious denominations except the Presbyterians.

The Country North of the Allegany and Ohio Rivers to Lake Erie, and New York line, bounded West by the State of Ohio, comprises the following

Counties.	Inhab.	Presbyterians.			Methodists.	
		Min	Ch. sup	Vac. So.	Itin.	Mem
Butler,	7,346	3	4	5		
Beaver,	12,168	3	7	7	1	436
Mercer,	8,277	8	12	4		
Crawford,	6,178	3	6	4		
Erie,	3,758	1	3	4	2	585
Total,	37,727	18	32	24	3	1021
Total W. of Allegany in Penn.	195,529	57	101	48	12	3787

These five counties it appears have 37 727 inhabitants; of the Presbyterian order, there are 18 preachers, 32 churches supplied by them, and 24 vacant societies. Some of these preachers are infirm and have no particular charge; others, though they live in this district, preach in Ohio. Some also are engaged in other business, and serve only as occasional supplies. This statement of the number of churches may not be perfectly accurate, because the different counties have many places of the same name. The Methodists have two circuits through this region, three itinerants in them, and 1,021 members in their communion. There is in the county of Butler or Beaver a society of Germans, who have all things common, and are remarkable for their industry, sobriety, and order. They have a preacher of their connection with them, a man advanced in life, and very zealous in directing their attention to divine things, for which purpose they meet daily. What is the name, or what are the peculiar sentiments of this society, I know not. The Methodists, for a time, were very successful, and broke up some Presbyterian societies. Of late they have not been so successful in this region.

This part of the country is a proper field for missionary labor. At least two profitable circuits for a mission might be established in the western part of Pennsylvania. The first through the counties on the Allegany River, begining with Armstrong Venango, and Warren, and returning through the parts of Erie, Crawford, Mercer, and Butler, by which the destitute places in those counties might be visited. The other through the counties of Cambria, Indiana, Clearfield, and Tyoga, and return through parts of Lycoming, Centre, and Huntingdon. The three last counties are East of the Allegany Ridge, contain 86,000 inhabitants, and have not one Presbyterian minister among them.

The people in the western parts of Pennsylvania are a medley of Scotch, Irish, English, and Germans. The Germans are few. The majority are of Scotch—Irish descent, many of them rude in their manners, but desirous to instruct their children. Schools

however, in the districts first and last mentioned, are not numerous. There are some good schools in Pittsburg, which is the
most flourishing pl-ce in the western country. In Washington
county are two Colleges, within ten miles of each other, both of
which have proved great blessings, by the facilities they afford to
acquire the rudiments of an education. The teachers of these
Colleges are pious men, and a great object with them ever has
been, to prepare young men for the gospel ministry. In this they
have been very successful, for most of the young men in the ministry, in these parts. h ve been educated in these Seminaries.

In September, 1812, the Synod of Pittsburg held their annual
meeting. From the Reports to the Synod, it appeared that it
was composed of the following Presbyteries:

Ohio, consisting of 23 Ministers, 38 Congregations, & 1 Licentiate.
Redstone,   17   37
Erie,   15   34   1
Hartford,   11   36   2
New Lancaster,   9   29   1

The two last Presbyteries, and part of Ohio, are in the State of
Ohio. Nothing particularly interesting was brought before the
Synod. The subject of atonement, as to its nature and extent,
has agitated the members of this Body some ; a majority of
whom, I think, embrace the opinions of Scott and Fuller. They
are uniform in administering the ordinance of Baptism to
none but professed believers and their households, and in requiring fruits meet for repentance, as necessary to admission into
their communion. From the Report of Synod it appears, that
the profanation of the Sabbath, by travelling, visiting, hunting,
fishing, &c is very common, and that profanity and intemperance
have become crying sins ; that altho' there was no special attention to religion, still many were brought into the kingdom of
Christ ; and that those who were admitted formerly remained
stedfast, adorning their profession. In no part of the western
country are the Presbyterian Churches in a more prosperous state,
or have been more remarkably blessed by the effusions of the
Spirit, than within the bounds of this Synod. It is now almost
thirty-four years since John Mc. Milian, D. D. the father of the
churches in these parts. first passed over the mountains. As we
were crossing the Allegany river, he expressed himself very feel-
ingly in the language of Jacob : *With my staff passed I over this
Jordan, and now I have become many bands*, alluding to the number of Presbyteries in union with this Synod. This Synod is a
Missionary Body and expends annually about $1,000. This has
however, been chiefly expended among the Wayandot Indians.
They send missionaries for a few weeks or months into different
parts within the bounds of their Synod.

NEW VIRGINIA.

The Blue Ridge, which divides the waters of James River and the others which fall into the Atlantic, from those of the Shenandoah, which empties into the Potowmac, separates Old, from New Virginia.

The land of this district, situated west of the Allegany Mountains, which divide the waters flowing into the Atlantic, from those which fall into the Ohio, is very broken and mountainous; though the vallies are fertile, and make excellent plantations. Between the Blue Ridge and the Allegany Mountains is an extensive, fertile, and highly cultivated body of land, and some parts of it, bordering on the Potowmac, are called the garden of America. Many of the inhabitants of New Virginia, are from the old settlements in that State. But a great part of them from Pennsylvania and Maryland, of the German and Scotch—Irish descent. The settlements west of the Allegany Mountains are very scattering, being confined chiefly to the water-courses and valleys. Those between the north and south mountains, that is in the valley just described, are numerous and flourishing, and the state of society is better and more improved, than in Old Virginia.

The District of Country in this State between the Allegany Mountain and Ohio River comprises the following

Counties.	Inhab.	Presbyterians.			Baptists.		Methodists.	
		Min.	Ch. Sup.	Va. So.	Ch.	Mem.	Tra.	Mem.
Brooke,	5,843		1				2	630
Ohio,	8,175				1	104	1	249
Wood,	3,036						1	340
Mason,	1,991							
Cabell,	2,717						1	172
Wythe,	8,356			2	1	78	1	367
Washington,	12,136	2	4	1	4	197	1	476
Russell,	6,316				5	334		
Monroe,	5,444	} 1	1		1	61	1	320
Greenbrier,	9,914		1		3	94	1	358
Kanahwa,	3,866				5	178	1	356
Lee,	4,694				1	60		
Teazewell,	3,007							
Grayson,	4,941				3	180		
Harrison,	9,958				7	133		
Randolph,	2,858						1	350
Monongahela,	12,792				5	180	1	254
Montgomery,	8,409			2	6	217		
Total,	114,454	3	7	5	42	1886	12	3852

It appears from this Table that these counties contain 114,454 inhabitants, and only 3 Presbyterian ministers, 7 churches supplied with preaching, and 5 vacant societies. Two of these ministers are really worn out in the service, and it is doubtful whether any after them will be settled over their societies, from a prevailing unwillingness to support ministers. Here are at least 100,000 inhabitants without one solitary Presbyterian preacher among them. The Baptists have 42 churches in this region, and 1816 members in their communion. The Methodists have 12 itinerants, and 3,852 members in their society.

This certainly must be considered a field for missionary labor, though I think the prospect small indeed, as it respects the formation of societies and churches. The people are willing to hear, however, and we should hope great good might be done among them eventually by proper exertions. If the circuits hereafter proposed in the State of Ohio were adopted, the five first counties in the Table, which are situated on the River Ohio, would be principally supplied. Another good circuit might be formed through the counties on the Monongahela River, and one more still on the Kanahawa in Greenbriar. The Presbyterian settlers are few in comparison with the Baptists and Methodists, which constitute the great mass of the community.

The Valley between the Allegany and Blue Ridge, or the North and South Mountains, comprises the following

Counties.	Inhab.	Presbyterians.			Methodists.	
		Min.	Ch.Sup.	Vac. So.	Itin.	Mem.
Jefferson,	11,851		2	2		
Berkley,	11,479	1	3	1	2	980
Frederick,	22,574	4	4		1	150
Hampshire,	9,384	1	1			
Hardy,	5,525		1		1	573
Pendleton,	4,293				1	328
Shenandoah,	13,646					
Rockingham,	12,753	4	4		2	865
Augusta,	14,308	6	4	3	1	259
Bath,	4,837					
Rockbridge,	10,318	3	7			
Bottetour,	13,301	2		3	2	555
Total,	134,269	21	26	9	10	3,710

In these counties is a population of 134,269 inhabitants. There are 21 ministers, 26 churches supplied by them, and 9 vacant societies of the Presbyterians. The Methodists have 10 itinerants, and 3,710 members in their society. The Baptists are few, and in several of the counties are some German churches both of the Lutherans and Calvinists. The Presbyterian churches here are evidently in a more flourishing condition than in any other part of the Southern States. They are increasing, and are in little need of missionary aid. The counties of Jefferson, Berkley, Pendleton, Shenandoah, and Rockingham, may however be con-

B

sidered missionary ground. I was not able to obtain accurate information respecting the number of Baptist churches in this district. They are however few.

In Old Virginia, are 16 ministers, and 23 churches supplied by
Presbyterian preachers. These are in the counties of Loudon,
Stafford, Spottsylvania, Amherst, Albemarle, Hanover, Gouch-
land, Norfolk, Dinwiddie, Cumberland, Prince Edward, Char-
lotte, Campbell, and Bedford. In all the other counties there
are none.

The Episcopal church is in a deplorable condition. The number of clergy small, perhaps between 20 and 30 and their churches about 100. The inhabitants of Old Virginia are nominally
Episcopalian, among the higher class of society. The Baptists
and Methodists are far the most numerous, but chiefly among the
lower class.

There appears to be a great opening for the Presbyterians at
present. The better informed are displeased with the Baptists
and Methodists, and though educated Episcopalians, seeing no
prospect of supply from that denomination, would cheerfully contribute to the support of a Presbyterian minister. There are a
number of applications to Presbytery for supply, but they have
no one to send.

Many young men have lately been stationed at some of the principal places in the State, and meet with great respect, and the attention of many appears to be called to divine things. They want
missionaries of talents, good address, fluency of speech, and easy
manners, as well as fervent piety. In this State, a missionary body, who collect $1,000 annually, have to place a great part of it to
interest or let it lie dormant, for the want of missionaries of proper
character to engage in their service.

OHIO.

NEW CONNECTICUT.

This district is situated between the 41° N. L. and Lake Erie,
and extends west from Pennsylvania State line, to a line drawn from
the 41° N. L. due North till it intersects Sandusky Bay, about
the centre, from East to West. The settlements at present however do not extend west of Cayahoga River.

Counties.	Inhab.	Presbyterians.			Methodists.	
		Min.	Ch. Sup.	Vac. So.	Itin.	Mem.
Ashtabula,	} 8,671	2	3			
Trumbull,		5	10	5	2	422
Geauga,	2.917	1	2	1		
Portage,	2.995	1	1	4		
Cayahoga,	1,459	1	1			
Total,	16,042	10	17	10	2	422

This portion of country in 1810 had 16,042 inhabitants, but will admit of a very extensive population, and in all probability, should peace be soon restored, will fill up with unexampled rapidity. This is not the case with this district only, but with the State generally, as also Indiana and Illinois Territories. For the war has brought into those parts hundreds and thousands from other States, where the soil is inferior and land so high, that it is impossible for poor people to purchase. These circumstances will render the country which they behold very desirable, and induce them to immigrate to it.

In New Connecticut are 10 preachers and 17 churches supplied with preaching, at least part of the time, and 10 vacant congregations. The Presbyterians are by far the most numerous. The Baptists are very few, and the Methodists have only one circuit and two preachers in the whole of the district. They are not encouraged by the better informed and most influential class of community. Many if not most of the inhabitants are from Connecticut and Massachusetts. They are well informed and, with some exceptions, their manners are less vicious than in the new countries generally. Missionaries are treated with respect, and heard with attention. The people are very desirous in many places, not only to have occasional preaching but to have Gospel Ministers settled among them. The Missionary Society of Connecticut have turned their particular attention to this district. They have 11 missionaries there who labor a part of the time in their service, and the residue they are supported by the people. The Lord has been pleased to pour out his Spirit here, and a revival of religion has taken place in some counties from which the happiest effects are likely to result. Some of the most influential characters, who were Infidels before, have been brought to acknowledge Christ. Many churches have already been formed, and many more might be organized ; two or three of which uniting could afford an adequate support to a minister.

The District of Country South of New Connecticut between Ohio River and the Muskingum and its waters, comprises the following

Counties.	Inhab.	Presbyterians.			Methodists.	
		Min.	Ch. Sup	Vac So.	Itin	Mem.
Columbiana,	10,878	3	3	1		
Jefferson,	17,260	5	5	2	1	1,155
Belmont,	11,097	1	1	2		
Washington,	5,991	3	5	3	2	306
Guernsey,	3,051			3	1	467
Muskingum,	8,500	1	2	3		
Tuscaraweis,	2,045				1	142
Stark,	2,734					
Total,	61,556	13	16	14	5	2,070

The population, except in counties bordering on the Ohio, is small and scattered. The soil is inferior in general, except the bottoms on the rivers, to the other portions of this State, and probably will not settle very rapidly. The settlements at present are chiefly confined to the water courses. The inhabitants of this district are 61,556; the Presbyterian ministers 13, and those chiefly in the villages; the churches supplied with preaching 16, and the vacant congregations 14. The Methodists have 5 circuit preachers, and 2,670 members in society. There are also a few Baptists here, but as to the number of their churches and ministers, I have no information. In the county of Jefferson there is a large settlement of Quakers. There are also several Halcyons in this part of the country, particularly at Marietta; and it is probable that the other denominations are far more numerous in this district than the Presbyterians. The better informed and influential men, however, even among the irreligious, prefer the Presbyterian order. The Synod of Pittsburg generally send one or two missionaries to labor in this district of country, two or three months in the year. The Missionary Society of Connecticut, also employ one or two missionaries for a few weeks. This district of country is in great want of missionary labor, for from Steubenville to Marietta along the Ohio, there is no Presbyterian preacher, and the settlements are numerous. So also after you leave Marietta up the Muskingum to Zanesville, there are none; and from thence to the head of the river through Tuscarawies and Steuben there are none. Through these places however, the Methodists have their circuits. In Tuscarawies county the Moravians have a mission among a few Indians, and others of their connection settled near them. The Indians are very dissipated and greatly degenerated since the time that Loskiel gives an account of them.

There are some Deists in almost every part of the country, many however are very silent and say little. I found some of these on the Muskingum. one of whom has lately been brought to see and acknowledge the error of his ways.

I cannot ascertain that there has been any revival of religion lately in any part of this district. The people are loose in morals; the profanation of the Lord's day, swearing and drunkenness, together with horse-racing and gambling, are very common. Two missionary circuits might be profitably established in this region. The first from Wheeling on both sides of the Ohio to Marietta, and for a short distance up Captine Creek and Muskingum River. The other on Will's Creek in Guernsey county, which is wholly destitute, and up the Muskingum above Zanesville. through Tuscaraweis and Stark counties, in which there are some places that have applied to Presbytery for supply. It is very probable that a number of churches might be organized in different parts of this district, was there particular attention paid to the subject. The ministers who are already in the country, it will hereafter appear, have no leisure to attend to it. It can be done therefore by missionaries only.

The District of Country between Muskingum River and the Sciota and its branches, and the Ohio River and New Connecticut, has the following

Counties.	Inhab.	Presbyterians.			Methodists.	
		Min.	Ch.Sup.	Vac. So.	Itin.	Mem.
Athens,	2,791	1	1	1		
Gallia,	4,181		1	1		
Sciota,	3.399				1	911
Ross,	15,514	3	6	2		
Pichaway,	7,124	2	2	1	1	769
Fairfield,	11,361	2	4	2	3	457
Licking,	3.852	2	4			
Coshocton,	1.536				1	210
Wayne,	1,000					
Richland,	1.000					
Knox,	2.149	1	3		1	508
Delaware,	2,000	2	2	2	1	345
Franklin,	3.486	1	2	2		
Madison,	1.605			1	2	124
Fayette,	1,854			1		
Total,	62,850	14	25	13	10	3,324

A great part of this district is very fertile; immigration to it has been rapid, and it will soon contain an extensive population. The number of inhabitants 62,850, the Presbyterian preachers 14, churches supplied with preaching are 25, and the vacant congregations 13. The Methodists have 7 circuits in whole or in part, in this district, 10 circuit riders, and 3,324 members of their society. They are probably, the most numerous of any denomination. In Fairfield county are several German societies of different denominations. In Gallia county is a society of Baptists, and also in Knox county.

This is a proper field for missionary labor. Many places in Madison, Fayette, and Sciota counties have made particular request to Presbytery for supply, and intimated a desire to settle a minister.

In Gallia county, there is a place where a preacher, who would take the charge of an Academy, would have a good support, and the prospect of usefulness is great. This place is settled by many French people, ignorant of all religion, and without a Bible. They are very dissipated and spend the Sabbath in dancing and other amusements, which argue that they hold it in sovereign contempt. A pious man, who sometime since removed there, opened a meeting on the Sabbath, at which he prayed and read a sermon, and has been the means, at least externally, of a great reformation in manners among them. There is also an opening for settlement in Sciota county, at Alexandria and Portsmouth. In Delaware county, at Bixbie settlement and Worthington, the inhabitants are from New-England Several other places are anxious to have stated preaching ; and by particular attention to the subject, many societies in different parts might be formed.

There has been of late considerable attention to religion on Leading Creek, in Gallia county, also in Knox county, under the preaching of Mr. Scott. There has also been a pleasing attention, particularly among the young people, on Rush Creek, and Mount-Pleasant in Pichaway county, under Mr. Robinson ; and also in Licking county, under Mr. Harris.

This part of the country is but little visited by missionaries. Those that have been employed here, were supported by the Missionary Society of Connecticut. This district may be divided into two circuits. First, on both sides of the Muskingum to Sciota River, and up the same to the Salt creek, in Ross county, and from thence through the country to Galliopolis by the Salt Works. The second, through the counties of Coshocton, Wayne, Richmond, Knox, part of Delaware, and Licking.

The Country comprised between the Sciota and the Little Miami, and heads of the Big Miami, and from the Ohio River north, to the Indian boundary line, has the following Counties, &c.

Counties.	Inhab	Presbyterians.			Methodists.	
		Min.	Ch. Sup	Vac. So.	Itin.	Mem.
Adams,	9,434	1	2		1	694
Highland,	5,766	1	3	1		
Clermont,	9,965				2	1,073
Clinton,	2,674					
Warren,	9,925	1	3	2		
Green,	5,870	1	2	3	2	641
Champaign,	6,303	3	3	1		
Total,	49,937	7	13	7	5	2,408

This is a very valuable tract of land, and is chiefly in what is called the Virginia military lands. The immigration to it before the war was rapid, and it will admit from the nature and situation of the country, a very extensive population. The inhabitants are 49,937. The Presbyterian ministers 7, churches supplied with preaching 13, and the vacant congregations 7. The Methodists are by far the most numerous, they have 5 circuit preachers, and 2,408 members of society. On the Sciota River, and west of it to the State line, is the principal seat of the Methodists in this State. There are also several New Lights in this part of the country, there is one preacher of theirs in Highland, three in Madison, and one in Champaign county. In the last named county there are 3 Baptist societies and one church. In this district are some other Sectaries headed by raving enthusiasts, which must expire with them, and are therefore unworthy of notice. There is a large settlement of Quakers in Highland county, and in Warren at Lebanon a settlement of 4, or 500 Shakers, headed by two or three that were formerly Presbyterian ministers. In Champaign county, on Kings creek, and Harmony, there is a number of Universalists. In this county formerly the New Lights were numerous, at present they are nearly extinct, being blended with the Methodists or Baptists. There are some still at Springfield.

Drunkenness and profane swearing are very prevalent in this district, and the Sabbath is greatly polluted, by visiting, hunting, fishing, and neglecting public worship even where they can enjoy it. This is a good field for missionary labor. In many parts there are settlements of Presbyterians that are anxious to have preaching, and although there are many of other denominations they will go to hear a missionary, and generally behave themselves with propriety, except that there is some occasional interruption from their groanings and crying, which the preacher may soon stop by adverting in prayer or address to some of the distinguishing doctrines which they reject. Preachers are no longer subject to interruption from them in their sermons, as was formerly the case when they first began to spread through the country. This part of the country is but little visited by missionaries. Those who have been here have generally been employed by the Synod of Pittsburg, or by the General Assembly There are neighborhoods which might soon be organized into societies, though they might not be able immediately to support preaching, owing to the divisions among the people. As society improves, these divisions, which arise perhaps from having emigrated from different parts will be done away.

The District of Country which is situated on the waters of the Big Miami, and west of it to the Indiana east line, contains the following Counties, &c.

Counties.	Inhab.	Presbyterians.			Methodists.	
		Min.	Ch. Sup.	Vac. So.	Itin.	Mem.
Hamilton,	15,258	2	2		} 3	817
Butler,	11,150	2	4	1		
Montgomery,	7,722	1	1			
Preble,	8,304			1	1	217
Miami,	} 3,941					
Dark,						
Total,	41,375	5	7	2	4	1,034
Total in Ohio.	231,760	49	78	46	26	9,258

This district, with the counties of Warren, Green, and Champaign in the district last mentioned, is far the best part of Ohio, both in soil and situation. Cincinnati, in particular, is the pleasantest situated town in the western country,—has considerable trade and a large population, nearly 2,000. The country has settled rapidly, and in a few years of peace and prosperity would be very populous.

The inhabitants of this district are 41,375 ; the Presbyterian preachers 5, churches supplied 7, and vacancies 2. The Methodists have a part of several circuits through it, about 4 itinerants, that ride circuit, and 1,034 members in their society. The Baptists have perhaps as many as 10 societies ; of them however I am not correctly advertised. This was formerly the seat of the New Lights. They are now dwindling away. Many of the better part of the preachers, as well as people, have seen and acknowledged their errors, and have returned to the Presbyterian church. Some have joined the Methodists, and ere long, probably, the name alone will remain. There are some Infidels, and their brethren the Universalists, all scattered in different places. There are also a few Halcyons and Swedenburgers, and one New Light in Butler county. In Preble, are two New Light preachers, and one in Miami county.

This is a district which stands in great need of missionary labors. Here might be many societies soon organized, and some of them, if the people would unite, could support a minister. The counties of Preble, Dark, and Miami are wholly destitute of preaching, excepting by a few New Lights, and some Methodists. Butler and Montgomery have only three preachers ; and many of these places have had but little attention from missionary societies. The wild enthusiasm, which raged through these parts a few years ago, was a discouragement to missions among them ; for no regular preacher could pass by without reproving many things, which would bring on him immediate persecution. Here is a great variety of religious opinions, a number of Arminians and Socinians ; for the New Lights are all Socinians, as will hereafter appear.

This with the former district will afford two good circuits. One down the Ohio, on both sides, as low as Big Miami ; the other through the counties of Champaign, Miami, Dark, Preble, Montgomery, and Greene. This last circuit, Mr. James Hughes, who has lately removed to Urbana, Champaign county, would be willing to undertake.

There has been some attention to religion in these parts, particularly at Buck creek, Champaign county, where there is a small Presbyterian society. It originated from a meeting which some pious people conducted, for they had no preacher. The manner of conducting these meetings was by reading the scriptures, a sermon, and singing and prayer. There has also been some attention in Butler county. The Methodists say there has been a very great revival of religion among them, as also do the Baptists, and that their numbers have doubled within the last year in Miami district. From the best information that could be obtained from eye witnesses of this work, there is great reason to believe, that it was principally terror and fear which induced numbers to join these societies; for this work began and ended with the earthquakes, in those countries; and the whole strain of preaching by the Baptists and Methodists was, that the end all things was at hand, and if the people were not baptized, or did not join society, there was no hope for them. This may be deemed uncharitable by some, but not when it is considered, that the Methodists in that region require no evidence of holiness of heart to become members of their society, and that the religious experiences of many consist only in dreams and visions, or the remarkable suggestion of some alarming texts of Scripture, and after that some which afford great comfort. It is also a fact that many, who joined their societies during the earthquakes, have already left them. Some have been excluded from their communion, and others are under censure. It must not however be understood that there were not among the number some subjects of real conversion. But the work as a whole is not entitled to be called a great revival of religion.

The inhabitants of the State of Ohio are emigrants from the different States in the Union, and cannot be said, as yet, to have formed a distinct character. These from New England, have carried with them the habits, and a love for the institutions, of their native States. We find them indulging the same independence in thought and actions, cherishing the same love of order, civil and religious, and expressing the same anxiety for the improvement of society, by the establishment of schools, and the ordinances of the gospel. Those from New Jersey and Pennsylvania, particularly of the Scotch and Irish descent, are very ready to unite in promoting the establishment of schools, and in supporting the gospel. Whilst those of German extraction, together with emigrants from Maryland, Virginia, and Kentucky, are too frequently regardless of both, and too fondly cherish that high toned and licentious spirit, which will suffer neither contradiction nor opposition, and which is equally inconsistent with civil and religious order.

Schools are not generally established throughout the State, though they are introducing in many parts as rapidly as the scattered situation of the settlements will admit. They are generally found in the villages; and it must be confessed that the instructors, at least many of them, need to be instructed themselves, not only in knowledge, but also in manners and morals. In many places good and able teachers are much wanted, and would be well paid for their services. In this State, places have been designated for three Colleges; one in New Connecticut, one

C

in Athens county, and one in Preble. The building which was erected for the purpose of a College in New Connecticut has been destroyed by fire. The one in Athens is in operation under the charge of the Rev. Jacob Lindsley. This is endowed with a large tract of land, which is leased out, and would bring in considerable rent if punctually paid, which unhappily is not the case. It is feared, by the friends of this Institution, that while the present state of things continues, it will be so cramped as to destroy its usefulness. The Trustees of the College in Preble have not yet erected their building, nor have they funds to proceed, the income from their lands being of small account. The late Rev. John W. Brown, in a tour through the Northern and Eastern States, collected for the Trustees about $ 1,000 in money, and between 1, and 2,000 dollars in books.

The great body of inhabitants in this State, who are not professors of religion, are not fixed in their religious sentiments. The most intelligent generally give preference to the Presbyterian order, but multitudes probably would be Presbyterians, Baptists, or Methodists, according to the denomination of the preacher under whose instruction they received their first religious impressions.

In October, 1812, was formed the Ohio Bible Society, which has received the support of the pious of different denominations. During the last year, they have distributed upwards of seven hundred Bibles, two hundred of which were sent to them by the Connecticut Bible Society ; and at their last meeting they appointed three ministers, to ride through the State to preach on this subject, showing the importance and necessity of such an institution, and to solicit subscriptions and donations for the same.

KENTUCKY.

Mr. Mills and myself entered this State 28th November, and left it on the 26th December, 1812.

The District of Country between the Virginia line, Ohio and Licking Rivers comprises,

Counties.	Inhab	Presbyterians.			Baptists.		Methodists.	
		Min.	Ch. Sup.	Va. So.	Min	Ch.	Itin.	Mem.
Grenup,	2,369				1	3		
Mason,	12,459	1	1		3	6	2	587
Bracker,	5,706				1	3		
Campbell,	3,283				3	4		
Lewis,	2,357					1		
Fleming,	8,947	1	2		2	5	1	625
Floyd,	3,485				1	2	1	282
Total,	38,606	2	3		11	24	4	1,494

This is a very broken, mountainous country. The river bottoms, such as those on rivers in general, are of the first quality. The upland also is very fertile and rich. Its population, however, will not probably greatly increase from immigration to it. The inhabitants are 38,606. The Presbyterian preachers only 2, and churches supplied with preaching 3. Of the Baptists in this district I have no particular account, not having been able to procure the Minutes of their Association. From the best information, the estimate in the Statistical Table is probably correct, which is 11 preachers, and 24 churches. The Methodists have 4 circuit riders in their bounds, and 1,494 members belonging to their society. There are also two New Light preachers and a few people of their denomination.

This region is seldom visited by Missionaries, nor is there any great prospect of forming Presbyterian churches, the greatest part of the people being Baptists or Methodists, and extremely bigoted. The circuit proposed through the two last districts in Ohio, would also embrace the settlements on the river in this district, and which in fact are the most important.

The District of Country between the Licking and Kentucky Rivers has the following Counties, &c.

Counties.	Inhab.	Presbyterians.			Baptists.		Methodists.		N. Lights.	
		Min.	C.S.	V.S.	Pre.	Ch.	Itin.	Mem.	M.	Ch.
Boone,	3,608			1	4	6				
Pendleton,	3,065				4	7	1	351		
Harrison,	7,752			3	5	10			1	1
Nicholas,	4,898	1	1	1	4	8				
Bourbon,	18,009	2	5		3	7			3	2
Bath,	} 12,975		1	1	3	5	} 2	930		
Montgomery,		1	1		3	7				
Estile,	2,082				1	3				3
Clarke,	11,519	1	1		2	6				
Fayette,	21,370	5	4	1	7	13	2	803	1	
Jessamine,	8,377	1	1	1	1	4				
Woodford,	9,655			2	2	4				
Scott,	12,419		1	1	5	9				
Franklin,	8,013	1	2		3	5				
Gallatin,	3,307				3	7				
Total,	127,049	12	17	11	50	101	5	2,084	5	6

This a tract of land which has rendered Kentucky so celebrated for the excellency of its soil; and the abundance of its crops is not exceeded, if equalled, by any portion of upland in our country. The population is already great, but will admit of a very great increase. It amounts at present to 127,049. There are 12 Presbyterian ministers, 17 churches are supplied, and there are 11 vacant congregations, which are able to support gospel ministers. The Baptists are very numerous, they have 50 preachers, and 101 churches. The Methodists have 5 circuit riders through this district, and 2.084 belonging to their communion. The New Lights have 5 preachers and 6 churches. The Episcopalians have 8 preachers and 2 societies, which are the only Episcopalian societies in this State. The Romanists have a chapel at Lexington, and another in Scott county.

This portion of the Vineyard is in great want of laborers, though it is visited every year for a few weeks by some of the missionaries under the direction of the General Assembly. The ministers that are settled have not leisure to devote that time to the attention of vacant congregations, and the formation of new societies, which is desirable, owing to their being obliged to spend a great part of their time in some worldly business, to support their families.

There is a prospect of forming churches, particularly at the county seats, which generally make application to Presbytery for supplies, if there were persons who would turn their attention to this subject. The generality of men of information prefer the Presbyterian order. It is however to be lamented, that there is a disposition to give up their opinions on this subject, and act against their better judgment, in order to secure popularity, and promote their interest.

The morals of the people are loose, and many of the inhabitants are extremely ignorant, as well as very vicious. The vices most prevalent are those which have been already mentioned, profanity, gambling, horse-racing, fighting, drunkenness, and violation of the Sabbath. They generally treat missionaries with respect; still there is not that regard for the clerical order among them, which is desirable. This arises from the principle of the Methodists and Baptists in selecting their preachers, and from the manners of the preachers themselves. Some short time since, the preaching of one of the missionaries of the General Assembly was greatly blessed among the Baptists in Boone county, and was the commencement of a considerable attention among them. There has also been a great stir among the Baptists and Methodists lately through this State generally.

In this part of the country are many Infidels. They are not so open and bold as formerly, and appear to carry on a more covert attack. In 1812, no less than three Infidel publications issued from the press at Lexington; and some of them published by persons unknown. Of one of these publications some were elegantly bound, and presented to the Legislature. A gentleman, a professed Infidel, was about to establish a school on Neif's system, where youth are to stay from eight to twenty-one years, and thus be initiated into all the illusions of infidelity from their earliest infancy.

The District of Country situated between Kentucky and Green Rivers, comprises the following Counties, &c.

Counties.	Inhab.	Presbyterians				Baptists		Methodists.	
		Min.	Ch.	Sup.	Vac. So	Prea.	.	Itin.	Mea.
Henry,	6,777	1	1			8	6		
Shelby,	14,877	1	3		1	10	16.	1	900
Nelson,	14,078	1	2			2	4	2	366
Mercer,	12,630	2	2		3	1	3	2	560
Gerard,	9,186					3	5		
Green,	6,735	1	3			6	8	1	644
Washington,	13,248	1	2			1	2		
Harden,	7,531					3	13		
Grayson,	2,301					1	2		
Brackenridge,	3,430					1	3		
Ohio,	3,792						1	1	553
ullet,	4,311					1	2		
Jefferson,	13,399	2	3			5	4		
Lincoln.	8,676	1	2			1	3		
Total,	120,971	10	18		4	43	74	7	3,017

The soil of this district, for the space of 40 miles from the Ohio, is similar to that of the former district, mentioned as situated on the same river, and the land on the waters which fall into the Kentucky, resembles the soil opposite to it, on the east side of the river. The land on the waters which fall into Green River is a grade inferior to that just described. Still it will admit of a great increase of population.

The number of inhabitants is 120.971. The Presbyterian ministers are 10; the churches supplied by them 18, and the vacant congregations 4. The Baptists have 43 preachers, and 74 churches. The Methodists have 7 circuit riders, and 3,017 members belonging to their society. The Roman Catholics are also numerous in parts of this district. In Bairdstown, Nelson County, resides a Roman Catholic Bishop, Joseph Flaggett. He has with him four priests, Fenwick, Buden, Nericks, and Wilson. They have a College near Springfield, at which are about twelve young persons preparing to be priests. They are also erecting a Nunnery on Harden's Creek, Mercer county, about ten miles from Springfield. They have four Chapels in Nelson, four in Washington, one in Mercer, and one in Jefferson. It is said they are increasing. There are two societies of Shakers, one in Mercer, the other in Lincoln county, each consisting of about five hundred people. This district is visited seldom by missionaries, though it would appear by representation, that they are much needed. There are neighborhoods of Presbyterians in many counties anxious to have preaching. Some Presbyterian societies could also be formed, particularly in the county towns, for wherever you find men well informed there is a decided preference to that denomination, and rather than hear the Baptists and Methodists, generally, they attend no where, and the consequence is a gradual and total neglect of the Sabbath day. The vices before enumerated are also very prevalent in this district. The Baptists and Methodists say they have had a great revival among them. The remarks already made on the revival in Ohio, are applicable to this, as far as the earthquakes reached.

The Country situated at the head of Green River, and between the Kentucky and Cumberland Rivers, comprises the following

Counties.	Inhab.	Presbyterians.				Baptists.		Methodists.	
		Min.	Ch.Sup.	Vac.	So.Prea.	n.	Itin.	n.	
Madison,	15,540	3	1	2	4	9			
Casey,	3,285				1	3			
Clay,	2,898				2	4	1	150	
Knox,	5,875				2	5			
Rochastle,	1.731				2	3			
Pulaski,	6,897				2	6			
Wayne,	5,430			1	2	5	1	543	
Total,	41,656	3	1	3	15	35	2	693	

This is a very mountainous and broken country ; the soil not more than middling ; and the chief employment of the inhabitants is the manufacture of salt-petre, of which immense quantities are made in this and the next district, and also in Tennessee. This is not a very desirable part of the country to live in, and the population, which is now very small and scattered, in all probability, will not greatly or rapidly increase.

There are 41,656 inhabitants. The Presbyterian ministers are 3 ; one church is supplied, and 3 are vacant. It appears strange, that there should be 3 preachers, and but one church supplied. It needs an explanation. They only reside here, but supply churches in other counties. The Baptists have 15 preachers, and 35 churches. In this district, and in two or three adjoining counties, is also what is called the South Kentucky Association of Baptists. These are entirely Arians or Socinians in sentiment. They have 10 preachers, 28 churches, and 1,300 members in their connection. There are here also a few New Lights.

There is no prospect of forming churches here, owing to the divisions and dissenisons which exist among the people on religious matters, and a disposition, which is very common where Baptists and Methodists are prevalent, an unwillingness to support the Gospel. The great mass of the people are very rude, ignorant, and vicious. It is possible, if a good missionary were sent among them, that he would be heard with attention.

The District situated South and West of Green River, and extending to the State lines on the South and West, comprises

| Counties. | Inhab. | Presbyterians. | | | Baptists. | | Methodists. | | N. Lights. | |
		Min.	C.S	V.S.	Pre.	h.	Itin	Mem.	M.	Ch.
Cumberland,	6,191				5	6				
Adair,	6,011	1			2	4				
Barren,	11,286	1	2		7	15	1	580	1	
Warren,	11,937			4	5	12			1	2
Logan,	12,123	1	1	2	2	3			1	3
Butler,	2,181		1		2	2			1	2
Christian,	11,020	1	2	3	2	4	1	200	1	2
Mughlenberg,	4,181			2	2	4				
Hopkins,	2,964		1		1	2				
Henderson,	} 4,703	1	2		} 1	2	1	175		
Union,		1	1							
Caldwell,	4,268	1	2		2	3				
Livingston,	3,674	1	1	1	1	2		615		
Total,	80,539	8	13	12	30	59	4	1,570	5	9

This part of Kentucky is denominated Barrens. Formerly there was scarcely any kind of timber on it, except in small spots. At present a great part of it is covered with shrub oak : the soil is very light and poor, otherwise the land is pleasantly situated, being very rolling. The population is scattered, being chiefly confined to spots, where there are timber and water, for it is very difficult to procure water by digging. The population will probably not greatly increase. Below Green River on the Ohio, the land is not broken, as on the upper part of the river.

There are 80,539 inhabitants. The Presbyterian ministers are 8, the churches supplied by them 13, the vacant societies 12. The Baptist preachers 30, and their churches 59. The Methodists have 4 circuit riders in this district, and 1,570 members of society. The Cumberland Presbytery have 4 or 6 preachers, and about 10 churches, besides several places of preaching. There are some New Lights here. There is also a society or two of Dunkers, who hold to the doctrine of the Universalists.

The General Assembly sends a missionary into this part of the country, to labor a few weeks annually. The people are very desirous to be visited by regular ministers, and treat such missionaries with respect and attention. There has been a great number of applications from this district to Mughlenberg Presbytery for supply. There is scarcely a county seat, which has not applied, and some of them are able and also anxious to settle a Presbyterian minister. The sentiments of many of the people are Arminian; the greater part however, have no fixed opinions or principles ; and it is a lamentable case, that many of them are regardless of religion, while others are blown about " by every wind of doctrine." The Baptists and Methodists have had a great increase of numbers to their respective societies. There has been no particular attention among the Presbyterians. The morals of the people are very lax. They appear totally regardless of the Sabbath.

The short time I spent in this State renders it impossible to point out any missionary circuit. It is recommended to Missionary Societies, to direct their missionaries to consult the Presbyteries in whose bounds they propose to labor, for information, as to the places which promise most success

The inhabitants of Kentucky are chiefly from Virginia, though there are emigrants from almost every State in the Union, and every Kingdom in Europe; these however bear but a small proportion to the whole population. Many of the earlier, as well as later settlers, were men of great respectability and weight of character, and their influence has had a good effect on the circle around them. The great mass of the people, however, were ignorant, poor, and vicious, and have handed to their descendants their feelings and habits. Before a regular government is established in a new country, a certain class of society is too much in the habit of doing that which is right in their own eyes, without regard to the actions, feelings, or interests of others.

Except in the villages, which are sinks of iniquity, there are very few schools established, throughout the State. The Legislature have endeavored to make some provision for the establishment of Academies, in the different counties, and for this purpose have granted 6,000 acres of land west of Green River, to each county. This land is worth from fifty cents, to one dollar per acre, but very little benefit has yet been realized from it. At Lexington is a College established, which has perhaps fifty students. It is not in a flourishing condition. Its funds are nearly $ 3,000 annually.

TENNESSEE.

This State is divided by the Cumberland Mountains into East and West Tennessee. Half, if not five eights, of the land in this State is claimed by the Cherokee and Chickasaw Indians. The inhabitants are from the Carolinas and Kentucky chiefly, a few are from Virginia and Georgia.

EAST TENNESSEE.

The soil of this part of the State is light and poor, in comparison with what is denominated good land in the western country. The timber is chiefly oak, and great portions of it only shrub oak. The settlements are chiefly confined to the Holstein, Clinch, and French Broad Rivers, with their waters. The state of society is generally much more improved here than in West Tennessee, or Kentucky.

It comprises the following Counties, &c.

Counties.	Inhab.	Presbyterians.			Methodists.	
		Min.	Ch. Sup.	Vac. So.	Itin.	Mem.
Bledsoe, Rhea,	}2,504	1	1			
Roane,	5,581			2	1	351
Anderson,	3,959					
Clairborn,	4,798				1	600
Campbell,	2,668					
Knox,	10,170	4	8	1		
Sevier,	4,595			2	2	959
Cocke,	5,154					
Blunt,	8,839	1	1	2		
Granger,	6,397				2	581
Hawkins,	7,643			1	1	305
Sullivan,	6,847			1		
Washington,	7,740	1	2	1		
Carter,	4,190				1	187
Green,	9,713	1	1	1	1	473
Jefferson,	7,309	2	2			
Total,	98,107	10	15	11	9	3,456

It appears from the above Table, that the population of this district is 98,107. The Presbyterian ministers are 10; the churches supplied by them 15, and the vacant societies 11. The Methodist itinerants are 9, and the members of their society 3,456. In the first seven counties there are 14 Baptist preachers and 30 churches, and in the other counties 12 preachers and 25 churches: the particular number in each county I could not ascertain. The Baptists are the most numerous, and probably the Presbyterians next. The Presbyterians probably are loosing ground, for some of their most active and zealous preachers have removed to West Tennessee. Here are ten counties containing upwards of 50,000 inhabitants, without one Presbyterian preacher, and scarcely a church. The General Assembly sends a missionary here occasionally, to labor a few weeks; but as a great portion of his time is necessarily consumed in going and returning, very little benefit can result from such missions. It must be confessed that missionaries are much needed here; many churches might be organized, and societies formed, were there only persons who could devote themselves to this object. The ministers that have already settled here, have so scanty a support, that they have to resort to some other occupation than preaching to maintain their families.

Within a year a Missionary, Tract, and Bible Society, uniting all these objects, has been formed in this district. It is the first and only Missionary Body, except the Synod of Pittsburg, west.

D

of the Allegany, and promises to be a blessing to this part of the country. The Constitution is similar to that of the " Massachusetts Missionary Society." The following is an extract of a letter, received since my return, from Charles Coffin, D. D. President of Green College, East Tennessee.

" Having read Brother Emerson's ' Evangelical Primer,' I am anxious it may be distributed extensively throughout the bounds of East Tennessee Missionary Society. More especially, I wish the children of my congregation may all have them. You must know all the Bible and Tract Societies in the middle and northern States. It must therefore be in your power to help us materially, by procuring a number of these Catechisms, Bibles and Tracts on the most important subjects, for distribution : Family religion, the Sabbath and its duties, the baptismal covenant, the advantages of early piety, &c. &c.   are such as I should choose. My wish is that you would see what can be done for us, and communicate the result. I should anticipate great good, were the Massachusetts Missionary Society to turn their attention to this State.   I was one who assisted to organize it, and greatly rejoice in its increase.

" For our Society we expect more members than means. We have more ground than our missionaries can occupy, and we have reason to hope, that other Societies will aid us, and work with us, to the extent of their power. Dr. Morse, says, in his Geography, ' Tennessee does not yet seem to have developed its character.' Missionary means and exertions may have great influence in forming it."

WEST TENNESSEE.

The soil of West Tennessee is very excellent, particularly between the Cumberland and Duck Rivers, and west of Cumberland Mountains. Many portions of this district are equal to the best lands in Kentucky, and as a whole, it is not inferior to the land in that State. The settlements are chiefly confined to the east of Tennessee and north of Duck Rivers. There are however a few settlements on the south waters of the Duck, and the branches of Elk Rivers. This portion of country has increased rapidly in population within a few years, and in all probability will continue to increase.

West Tennessee contains the following

Counties.	Inhab.	Presbyterians.			Baptists.		Methodists.	
		Min.	C.S.	V.S.	Prea.	Ch.	Itin.	Mem.
Humphreys,	1,511				1	2		
Montgomery,	8,021			1	2	3	1	377
Robertson,	7,270			1	2	1		
Summer,	13,792	2	3		2	3		
Wilson,	11,952	2	4	2	5	5		
Smith,	11,649			1	3	7		
Overton,	5,643						2	803
Jackson,	5,401						1	710
Rutherford,	10,265			3	4	6		
White,	4,028			1				
Williamson,	13,153	1	1	3	3	4		
Davidson,	15,608	1	3	2	3	3	1	550
Dickson,	4,516			3	2	4	1	783
Stewart,	4,262			1	1	2	1	170
Hickman,	2,583			1	3	3	1	440
Maury,	10,359	4	8	5	3	3		
Bedford,	8,242			3				
Warren,	5,725			1				
Franklin,	5,730			1			2	625
Lincoln,	6,104	1	1	1				
Giles,	4,516			3				
Total.	160,360	11	20	33	34	46	10	4,458

From this Table it appears that the inhabitants of West Tennessee are 160,360; Presbyterian ministers 11, Churches supplied by them 20, and the vacant societies 33. The Baptists have 48 preachers and 71 churches, including, besides those mentioned in the above Table, an Association in the four counties last named, which consists of 14 preachers and 25 churches; the number in each county I could not ascertain. The Methodists have 10 itinerants, and 4,458 members in their society. There are also seven speakers belonging to the Cumberland Presbytery, and a few New Lights. It further appears, that there are fifteen counties containing nearly 100,000 inhabitants, without a single Presbyterian minister among them. It must be observed, however, that the Presbyterian church is increasing very rapidly in members and ministers, and were there preachers, many more churches might be formed. There is a pressing call to the Presbytery from the villages and towns, in every county for supply, and it is greatly to be regretted that they cannot be supplied with proper missionaries or ministers. Mr. Blackburne is of opinion, that a great number of churches might be organized, if there were a proper person employed in the business; and regrets that his time is so much occupied with his school, that he has no leisure to devote to this object. It would greatly promote religion if some

Missionary Body would employ this man in their service, permitting him at the same time to supply his own societies. The more intelligent and enlightened people are decidedly in favor of Presbyterianism, and missionaries are treated with respect and heard with attention. These men too, will rather spend the Sabbath at the tavern, or riding and visiting for their amusement, than attend the preaching of Baptists or Methodists.

The state of society in this country is poor, and has made little advancement, as is the case in all new countries, for the lower class of people, who are very rude, ignorant, and vicious, constitute the mass of population. There are, however, in almost every county, some very respectable families from the Atlantic States. The vices most prevalent are intemperance, profanity, and violation of the Sabbath, gambling, duelling, and horse-racing.

Schools are established in the villages about the country, but few in the country settlements, and perhaps the great body of the people do not encourage them. There are two Colleges, one in East Tennessee, at Knoxville, and one in West Tennessee, at Nashville, endowed by the United States with 50,000 acres of land, which has been sold at one dollar per acre. The one in West Tennessee is in operation, and has between forty and fifty students. The College at Knoxville is not yet erected. In East Tennessee are two other Colleges, one in Washington county, of which the Rev. Mr. Daak is President ; and one in Green county, at the head of which is the Rev. Charles Coffin, D. D. These two Colleges have been great blessings to the State, and at them many of the physicians, lawyers, and ministers in that part of the country were educated. At the College in Green are five young men preparing for the ministry. Congress has also appropriated 100,000 acres of land for the purpose of establishing Academies in each county. Many of these are already in operation, and have more students than their Colleges, and as good instructors.

MISSISIPPI TERRITORY.

The soil of this Territory is various, from the very best to the very poorest. The upper part of the Territory, as low as Yazoo River, is much of it very good. From the Yazoo to the line of demarkation, the good land extends only a few miles from the Missisippi, until it is interrupted by broken land, which extends twenty or thirty miles in breadth, and beyond that is a poor light soil. The timber is long leaf pine, which extends to Tombigby and Mobile Rivers, and south through West Florida to the Gulph, in which tract there is no good land except on the water courses. It is estimated that not more than three eighths of this large tract of country will answer for cultivation, either from the barren, swampy, or broken state of the country.

Three-fourths of this Territory are still claimed by the Chocktaws, Chickesaws, Cherokee, and Creek Indians. The settlements are few, and many of them very scattering. On the Missisippi, they begin at the mouth of the Yazoo, and extend for a few miles from the River to the line of demarkation, and along this line east to Mobile, and up Mobile and Tombigby, in the forks of Alabama, a few miles above St. Stephens. There is also one county, *viz.* Madison, north of Tennessee River.

This Territory contains the following Counties, &c.

Counties.	Inhab.	Presbyterians.			Methodists.	
		Min.	Ch. Sup	Vac. So.	Itin.	Mem.
Warren,	1,114					
Clairborne,	3,102		1		} 1	149
Jefferson,	4,001	1	1			
Adams,	10,002	2	2		2	186
Wilkinson,	5,068	} 1	1		2	61
Amite,	4,750		1		1	170
Madison,	4,699				1	348
Washington,	2,920				2	140
Franklin,	2,016					
Wayne,	1,253					
Baldwin,*	1,427					
Total, Whites.	40,352	4	6		9	1,054
Slaves,	17.088					
Total, Inhab.	57,440					

From the preceding Table it appears that the population of this Territory is 57,440; Presbyterian churches 6, the ministers 4, the Methodists itinerants 9, members of society 1,054. Of the Baptists, there are in Madison county 2 preachers, and 5 churches. In the other counties there is an Association consisting of 11 preachers and 15 churches, and 494 members in their communion. The number of preachers and churches in each county I did not learn. It will also be seen that there are six counties, containing upwards of 14,000 inhabitants without one Presbyterian preacher. Of the four Presbyterian ministers, one is superannuated and without a charge. the other three are obliged to teach schools to support their families; so that the whole work of their ministry consists merely in preaching on the Sabbath. It must be confessed that every part of this Territory is a field for missionary labor, and it is thought that a few societies and churches might be organized, and that a zealous, faithful preacher, of engaging address, would obtain a handsome support.

* The five counties last named constitute the Mobile district.

The state of society in this Territory is truly deplorable. Most of the emigrants to this country came here for the purpose of amassing wealth, and that object seems to have absorbed their souls.

The schools are few and indifferent. At Washington is a College endowed with a large tract of land, but its income is small. One of the Presbyterian ministers has the charge of it.

A Bible Society has lately been organized at Natchez, is patronized by the influential men in the Territory, and promises utility.

INDIANA TERRITORY.

The soil of this territory is, in general, very excellent, particularly on the waters of the Big Miami, and White Rivers, the Wabash and its tributary streams. The poorest land, in this Teritory, is between the falls of Ohio and Anderson Rivers, being chiefly a hard gravelly soil, timbered with oak of small growth. The land between Anderson and Saline Rivers is chiefly good, but its situation, in general, is unhealthy. The best lands in this territory are still claimed by the Indians.

The settlements are on the Whitewater, and other branches of the Big Miami, and on the Ohio; between the falls of Ohio and Vincennes, there are a few houses. There are very flourishing settlements about Vincennes.

Indiana Territory contains the following Counties, &c.

Counties.	Inhab.	Baptists.		Methodist.		N.Lights.	
		Prea.	Ch.	Itin	Mem.	Prea.	
Franklin,	2,100	3	4	1	306	1	One Presbyterian in this County.
Wayne,	1,820	1	2			1	
Dearborn,	3,140	4	6	1	350	1	
Jefferson,	1,500	2	4			1	
Clarke,	4,450	2	5	1	381	1	
Harrison,	3,595	1	2			1	
Knox,*	7,645	1	6	2	173	1	
Total,	24.250	14	29	5	1,210	6	

In this district, containing a population of 24,250, the Baptists have 14 preachers and 29 churches; the Methodists have 5 itinerants and 1,210 members in their society, and there are 6 preachers of the New Lights. At Bussaron, not far from Vincennes was a Shaker settlement, but it has been lately broken up by the war. There is also a settlement of about 80 souls, of Switzers, from Vevey in the Pays de Vaud, near Geneva Lake, who speak the French language. These people are Calvinists in sentiment, and regret that they have no one to preach to them

* Knox county is on the Wabash, about Vincennes.

in their own language. By occupation they are vine dressers, and have about twenty acres of vineyard. At their vintage in 1811, they made 2,700 gallons of red wine, from the Cape grape, besides some from the Madeira grape. They are sober, industrious, and frugal, and though they have no minister, they meet together on the Sabbath, for the purpose of reading the Scriptures, a sermon, prayer, and singing. John James Dufour, a man of upwards of 80, a vine dresser of Vevey in Switzerland, who has seven children, six of whom are heads of families, in this colony, has sent a long epistle to them and the whole colony, on the different subjects of Theology, as a new-year's gift, and desired that they would read it frequently in their meetings on the Sabbath, but by all means, on every new-year's day, when all of them should assemble for that purpose. There is only one Presbyterian minister in this rapidly settling territory.

One great cause of the number of Baptists and Methodists in the western country is, that they direct their attention to places, which are rapidly settling, while in their infancy. If we wish to introduce correct sentiments, and Presbyterian churches, into Indiana, we must send missionaries there while the settlements are forming, for the people as a body when they immigrate to a place, are not fixed in their sentiments, but are eventually, what the preacher is, who is instrumental in calling their attention to the subject of religion.

ILLINOIS TERRITORY.

The settlements in this territory are very small and are much scattered. Those on the Ohio are few, except the Saline and Shaawnee town, and about fort Massac. On Cash River, is a small settlement, but the principal are about Kaskaskias on the Missisippi, at the American bottom.

This country is delightfully situated, as to climate and is almost a continued prairie, interspersed with copses of wood, from Vincennes to St. Louis. From a survey of a road between these two places, lately made, it appears that this distance of 150 miles, the country is for every half-mile, or mile, alternately prairie and open wood land. The American bottom is said to be the finest body of land to be found in the western country.

This Territory has only two counties at present,—Randolph containing 7,275 inhabitants, embracing the settlements on the Ohio and Kaskaskias; and St. Clair 5,007, embracing the settlements opposite St. Louis and Missouri, on the upper settlements. Of this county, Cahokia is the county town. In this whole Territory is not a solitary Presbyterian minister, though there are several families of this denomination in different settlements. At Kaskaskias they are anxious to obtain a Presbyterian preacher of proper character and talents, who would be willing to take the charge of an Academy. The Baptists have 4 or 5 small churches consisting of not more than 120 members. The Methodists have 5 itinerants, besides some local preachers, and perhaps 600 members in their society. This country was rapidly settling before the war, and should peace be restored, will greatly increase in population, and ought to receive early attention from Missionary Bodies.

MISSOURI TERRITORY.

This Territory is situated West of the Missisippi, and extends from the 33° N. L. North west to the boundaries of Louisania, which are indefinite and unsettled. The jurisdiction, however, of the Territory, does not extend beyond the limits of which the Indian claim is extinguished ; that is, from the mouth of the Jaflone on the Missisippi, to Charitous on the Missouri, and east of a line drawn from fort Ossage, 36 miles below the mouth of Kansas River, directly south to Arkansas. This line will also bound the settlements on the west ; for west of it commence extensive prairies, on which is no timber, except a small strip on the water courses, until near the heads of the Arkansas, Platte, Kansas, and Missouri Rivers.

The settlements are scattered, and confined almost entirely to the water courses. They extend up the Missouri about 25 miles; up the Merimeck some distance, and on the Missisippi to St. Genevieve. There is also a settlement of Germans on the heads of the St. Francis. There are no settlements of any consequence between the mouth of the Ohio and New Madrid. The other settlements are on Arkansas, about 50 miles from its mouth. There are also a few settlements on White River.

Counties.	Inhab.	Itin.	M.	Counties.	Inhab	Itin.	M.
Cape Girardien,	3,888		76	New Madrid,	2,103	1	50
St. Genevieve,	4,620	1		St. Francis,	0,188		
St. Louis,	5,657	2	147	Arkansas,	0,874		
St. Charles,	3,505	2	172				
Total,	17,660	5	395	Total,	3,165	1	50

The Country north of the mouth of the Ohio, comprises the following Districts : — *The Country south of the mouth of the Ohio, contains the following*

In the Territory contained in the two preceding Tables, the Baptists have 5 or 6 small churches, consisting of not more than 130 members. There is no Presbyterian minister. Of the population of this Territory, it is estimated that two-fifths are Americans, and the rest French. The Americans are chiefly of the lower class, and the people generally are extremely rude and ignorant, but few of the French can read. In fact they are much assimilated to the Indians, in love of indolence and hunting, rather than labor. It is probable that this country will settle very rapidly, for it is scarcely exceeded in America for climate, situation, and fertility of soil ; in the latter it is much like Kentucky.

The following is an extract of a letter, received from Stephen Hempsted of St. Louis, formerly from Connecticut :—" Since my residence here, in my excursions through the country, I endeavored to ascertain the religious sentiments of the inhabitants. I find there are more than 100 families who have been brought up Presbyterians, within the circuit of from five to fifteen miles, and who would readily contribute to the support of a Presbyterian preacher, who would occasionally visit them ; and many would constantly attend meeting at St. Louis. Many of my acquaintances have joined either the Baptists or Methodists, rather than live any longer without the ordinances and worship of God, and would gladly return to the Presbyterian churches, whenever they shall be organized. I have frequently heard the Baptists and Methodist preachers, and am acquainted with some, whom I have uniformly found without education, and of small talents. It appears to me, if a suitable Presbyterian minister should come here, in the present state of our Territory, that he would have large audiences, and be enabled, by the blessing of God, to plant a branch of the heavenly vine, which will one day extend over the whole of this Territory. I have frequently enquired of those who are possessed of information respecting the state of religion in general, in this and Illinois Territory, and have been informed that the Methodists, in both Territories, have nearly twenty local and itinerant preachers, and that the Baptists have ten small churches, containing not more than two hundred and seventy members ; that there are neither Presbyterian preachers nor churches in either Territory, though there are a few Presbyterian families in Illinois. I believe the formation of a Bible and Tract Society would be very useful here, for there are many who have not the means of procuring them if they were desirous to do it. I have distributed a few Tracts of my own that I brought with me, which were received with thankfulness, and I trust have done some good. If any of the Societies in New England will send on some Tracts and Bibles to my charge, I will distribute them among the poor and needy, who are famishing for the word of life.

" In my interviews with the heads of families and officers of government, they expressed a strong desire to have a Presbyterian minister of education, piety, morals, and talents, settled at St. Louis, and said that they would contribute liberally and continually to his support. They have frequently requested me to write to the Missionary Society of Connecticut to send them one, which I should have done this spring, had I not received your letter."

The Catholic priests are few, not to exceed three that officiate. I know of but one, he is at St. Genevieve and is said to be a very dissolute character.

F.

LOUISIANIA.

This State extends east to Pearl River, and from the Gulph, east side of the' Missisippi, to the 31° N. L. and on the west side of the River to the 33° N. L. and west to the Sabine, until it crosses the 32° N. L. and from thence with a line due north until it meets the 32° N. L.

The land east of Pearl River to the Perdido, and which formerly was a part of West Florida, is now comprehended in the Missisippi Territory. The land west of the Sabine, as far as our claims of Louisiania extend, is at present considered neutral territory ; between our government and Spain, the question of *right* concerning it is to be decided in future.

This State can only admit a very limited population, because the settlements must necessarily be confined to the water courses, the banks of which are considerably higher than the intervening country, in the valley of the Missisippi. Beyond this valley, the land is so poor as hardly to be capable of cultivation. This is particularly the case with West Florida, and the high lands on the west of the Missisippi, towards the Gulph, the soil of which is sandy, and the timber long leaf pine. The settlements, east of Lakes Maurepas and Bouchantrian to Pearl River, are few and scattering, but chiefly Americans. The settlements on the Missisippi are very flourishing, and from point Coupee, to some distance below New Orleans on both sides of the river, present almost a continued village. The inhabitants of the upper part of the settlements are from Canada, the middle, Germans, and in the lower part are French and Spanish from Europe. All speak the same language, and are similar in habits, manners, and religion. In the settlements of Atuckapas and Oppelousas, which are situated on the Gulph west of the Missisippi, are Spanish, French, and Americans. The settlement on Red River is principally French, and in the Washita, American.

The state of society in this country is very deplorable. The people are entirely ignorant of divine things, and have been taught only to attend mass, and count their beads. They are without schools, and of the French inhabitants, not one in ten can read. Their whole business seems to be, to make the most they can of their plantations. They are not intemperate. Continence is with them no virtue. The Sabbath to them is a high holiday, and on it, is committed, perhaps, more actual sin, than during the whole week besides. Dancing, gambling, parties of pleasure, theatrical amusements, dining parties. &c. &c. are the common business of the day, after mass in the morning. The religion professed in this country is entirely Roman Catholic. The clergy of this order, however, are not numerous, perhaps fifteen. The Bishop and four or five priests reside at New Orleans. Bishop De Burg appears to be a man of piety. He laments the degraded state of their church in Louisiania, and mourns over the depravity and wickedness of the place, in which he resides. The Bishop and Father Antonio favored the establishment of the Louisiania Bible Society, which will doubtless prove a long and lasting blessing to the State.

Last winter, perhaps for the first time, was New Orleans visited by Presbyterian missionaries. Our stay, though short, we hope will prove beneficial. Many were anxious to have the ordinances of the Gospel established, and desirous that I should abide with them. I regretted that it could not be so, for I believe the Lord has many people in that city; that it is an ample field for usefulness, and the most important in the western country. When Mr. Mills and myself arrived at New Orleans, we found there a Baptist and a Methodist missionary. The former left it in company with us, the latter would probably soon follow. He met with no encouraging prospects. A Presbyterian church may be established with a prospect of success in this place; and New Orleans ought to receive the attention of Missionary Societies.

This Territory has a population of 76,556 free people, and 34,660 slaves, not more than one-fourth, if one-sixth, are Americans. Among all these, there is not one Protestant church, unless it be a small one of Baptists, about to be organized in Oppelousas. The Methodists have had itinerants up Red River and Washita, but are exceedingly unpopular.

The government of this State is turning its attention to the establishment of Schools and Academies in different parts of the country; and at New Orleans have founded and endowed a College. These were very much needed, for we can expect to accomplish little in a missionary point of view among the French, until they are instructed, both in their own and in the English language. Much good might be anticipated from a protestant French missionary, if one could be sent among this people. We have reason to rejoice that the Lord has put it into the heart of our Bible Societies to send Christ and his apostles, Moses and the prophets to preach to them in their own language.

Having now exhibited the number of ministers and churches of the different denominations in the western States and Territories, together with a view of their population, it appears necessary to notice the character and sentiments of those preachers, and the discipline practised in those churches, to ascertain what attention this portion of our common country merits from Missionary Societies.

PRESBYTERIANS.

THE ministers of this denomination were few of them born in the western country, many of them are from Europe; but generally they are from the Atlantic states. They are men of correct morals and deportment; most of them have pursued a course of classical studies at the seminaries in the States, from which they emigrated, or in which they now reside. There is a departure from Presbyterian order in their settlements. Few indeed of them stand in the relation of pastor to the people among whom they labor. In general there is only an annual contract, between the minister and the people, at the expiration of which he may remove to another place, or the people make a contract with another minister to supply them for the year. The congregations are generally small on account of the great diversity of religious opinions, and from this, as from various other causes, are both unwilling and unable to give a minister an adequate support for his family. The consequence is that ministers are obliged to resort to some other employment for support. Those in villages, where they are generally located, take charge of schools; those in the country manage their farms, and some, thinking it more consistent with the ministerial character, become physicians. The evils resulting from these things are various and deplorable. The neglect of catechising the youth, family visitations, and a due preparation for the services of the sanctuary, is the most prominent. Catechetical instruction has always been the subject of sneer, ridicule, and hatred, among those, and those only, who are desirous of introducing error. It is owing to the neglect of this practice, more perhaps than to any other cause, that Errorists have been so successful in the western States. Christians ought not to be induced, by the sneers, ridicule, or sophisms of men whose great object is to make proselytes, to relinquish a practice, which has proved the most effectual means to establish the young and wavering from being carried " about by every wind of doctrine." Neither ought they tamely to suffer themselves to be seduced to believe, by men who would rob God of his glory, that those doctrines, which holy men of God have professed in view of the stake, and that too when the denial of these would have secured them the smiles and emoluments of the world, are of little consequence. It is by adopting such specious pretences as these, in the first place, that many whom we had reason to believe had tasted the good word of God, have been left to go on, step by step, until they have made shipwreck of their faith, and denied the Lord that bought them. Family visitations are also neglected in the western country for want of proper ministerial support. In conversation on this subject with the clergy, they seemed to insinuate, that it was not their duty, because they were not the pastors of the people. However this business may be managed to ease the conscience, the command of Christ to his ministers is, " feed my sheep....feed my lambs." This command cannot be fulfilled by ministers who know not the condition, views, and feelings of the people, which can be known only by being conversant with them in their families. Errorists make more proselytes by the fire side, than in their public discourses, and here is the place most effectually to answer objections, remove difficulties, give instruction to the weak, and confirm the doubtful.

The method of preaching is extemporaneous, frequently without writing, or meditation, it is rather exhortatory, than doctrinal. This arises from the worldly avocations of ministers during the week. This mode of preaching without writing, in most cases, even with those of good talents, and who once promised fair to rise in their profession, creates a sameness in their discourses. It is impossible for ministers thus situated to give that attention to vacant societies, and to the organization of churches, which is desirable in a new country, where settlements are rapidly increasing. If, however, Presbyterians are desirous of increasing the number of their churches, and disseminating correct sentiments; their attention ought to be directed to settlements in their infancy, before other denominations have organized their societies, and become firmly established. The Presbyterian ministers are mostly settled in the villages, of which there is generally, at least one in each county. The whole space of country around them is therefore the field for other sects. From all these considerations, it appears that the country is poorly supplied even where they have the best ministers.

The sentiments of the Presbyterians are conformable to their standards, in which, we believe, is taught the word of God. There is some diversity of opinion on the subject of atonement; some hold to limited atonement, and some believe in a general atonement, receiving it, as a governmental transaction, and not in the light of debt and credit. A majority of the clergy have embraced the former sentiments on this subject. For admission to their communion, they require scriptural evidence of a change of heart, a knowledge of the word of God, of the scheme of salvation through Christ, and a profession of faith in the doctrines of the Gospel, taught in their church. The churches are uniform in the practice of administering the ordinance of baptism to none but professing believers, and their households. The Lord's Supper is administered only twice in the year. On such occasions, it is customary for the neighboring ministers to assemble, and to hold meetings, at least three or four days in succession. This denomination is noted for their strict observance of the Sabbath; and the contrast between them and the sects who esteem all days alike, in this respect, is very great. They are the most intelligent part of community, lovers of order, and promoters of knowledge: the most ready to support schools, the Gospel, and Missionary and Bible Societies.

CUMBERLAND PRESBYTERY.

A Presbytery by this name was constituted in 1802, by the Synod of Kentucky. During the extraordinary revival of religion in this State, which commenced in 1797, and continued nearly ten years, while the people's feelings were made the test of good preaching, sound doctrine, and truth, many believing they had an immediate call to preach the Gospel gave public exhortations, and so much pleased the people, that they thought them divinely inspired. This Presbytery concluded, that education was not necessary in a gospel minister, and therefore licensed several of those young exhorters to preach. The Synod of Kentucky censured their proceedings, and dissolved them as a body. From this disunion of Synod, many of the Presbytery dissented ; some had always disapproved of licensing young men ; some turned Shakers ; and some formed themselves into an independent Presbytery, under the same name as the one dissolved by the Synod, and which is now to be noticed. The present Cumberland Presbytery has adopted the discipline and confession of the Presbyterian Church, with the exception of requiring an education in the candidate, in order to license him to preach, and the doctrine of divine decrees as there taught. From this it might easily be conjectured, what is indeed the fact, that they are illiterate themselves. Their moral character, as far as I could learn, stood perfectly fair. In sentiment, many of them do not materially differ from the Methodists, and it is not uncharitable to suppose that none of them have a consistent system of doctines. It is probable that the better part of these people will be eventually united to the Presbyterian church, and the remainder join the Methodists. As to their mode of preaching, it is very similar to that of the Baptists and Methodists, which will be presently described. Their mode of itinerating is something similar to that of the Methodists. In Kentucky and Tennessee, they have only 12 preachers and a few licentiates ; and have 90 different places of preaching, according to information received from one of their ministers in Tennessee.

BAPTISTS.

The preachers of this denomination are generally illiterate ; few are possessed of good common English learning, and there are also some, that can neither read the Scriptures, nor write their names. Learning, with them as a body, is rather ridiculed than desired ; and while they pretend to despise all human knowledge, they profess to be led and directed by the Holy Spirit, both in desiring the office of an elder, and in their public performances. The power of licensing lies wholly with the church, of which the person is a member, and the church are the only judges of the necessary qualifications. The common practice on the subject is this, the person makes a statement to the church, that he feels an inward call to preach the Gospel.—on this, the church, for fear lest they should be found fighting against the Spirit, generally permit him to exercise his *gifts*. If he is approved by them, he is soon ordained by the elders of the church. No specific time is necessa-

ry to intervene between his church-membership and ordination as
a preacher, and it happens in some churches that the time is short
indeed, perhaps three, or six months. In their manner of preaching, their object appears to be to excite the passions; to terrify
and raise into trasports of joy, rather than to inform the mind,
convince the understanding, convict the heart, and open the way
of salvation through Jesus Christ. To this end, they dwell much
on the torments of hell, while the spirituality and the obligation
of obedience to the law, and the justice of its penalty, are seldom
termed. The crucifixion of Christ is represented in the most
tragical manner, while the design of the sacrifice, viz. the mag-
nifying of the law, the display of God's hatred to sin, his justice,
the riches of his grace, the love of Christ, is frequently passed
over in silence. They often introduce tender stories, wonderful
dreams and visions, with such expressions of countenance, and
affecting tones of voice, as are calculated to excite the tender,
sympathetic emotions of the heart. There is also a studied sin-
gularity in the choice of their texts, and an effort to spiritualize
every passage of Scripture. The ordinance of baptism consti-
tutes the greater part of their discourses, or at least a portion of
each; and is insisted on in such a manner, as would induce the
belief that their peculiar mode of administering it is a necessary
qualification for admission into heaven, as well as to their communion. They pretend also to preach wholly by the Spirit, by
which they mean, as the Spirit gives them utterance, in the manner the apostles were inspired; and it very often happens, that
at the same meeting, many of them who pretend to preach by the
Spirit, contradict each other. This people do not distinguish
between the word Spirit, as used in different parts of the Scripture. It is frequently used as an agent, as in the texts where the
prophets and apostles are said to be inspired to reveal the will of
God, and where the renewing of the heart is mentioned. But
more commonly it signifies a holy disposition, produced by the
agent. In the first sense the Spirit is an infallible guide, but in
this manner he is not given to us, as he was to the prophets and
apostles. In the second sense, the Spirit is not given for the
guide of our actions, nor the rule of our faith, but to incline us to
walk in the ways of God's commandments, and to prepare us for
his holy presence. It is the mistaken notion of this Spirit that
has caused so much ignorance, error, and enthusiasm in the West;
for the *Spirit within*, as they term it, is made the guide of their
actions, and rule of their faith. If, for instance, they feel a desire to be preachers, they have a call of the Spirit. If they are
greatly impressed that certain practices are right, and others
wrong, it amounts to the authority of the Spirit, that the course
which the impressions direct, is correct. If they are highly ele-
vated, with agreeable and pleasant feelings, under the preaching
of certain doctrines and views of truth, they have the witness of
the Spirit within them, that the one is true and the other false.

These observations on the Spirit are applicable to several denominations. By this it may be perceived, that instead of following the doctrines of Christ, to try the Spirits by the law and testimony; they try the law and testimony by the *Spirit within*. It was from this delusion that all the fanaticism and enthusiasm sprung which overspread the western country a few years since, and produced a flood of error.

The term of admission into the Baptist church is a relation of their experiences. In these it is thought, too much attention is paid to feelings and impressions of the individuals without examining them by the word of God. Dreams, visions, the unusual suggestion of some text of Scripture, which are very alarming, and others that cause great inward joy and rejoicing, also form a great part of the experience.

In sentiment they are much divided. The better informed are Calvinists; but many are either Antinomians or Arminians. There are many Arians and Socinians, both of which, in some way or other, believe the doctrine of universal salvation. In some points they all agree, such as ministerial support, and the Sabbath., Against the salaries of ministers they are clamorous; and they denominate Presbyterian ministers. *fleecers of the flock.* As a body, they deny the morality of the Sabbath or Lord's day; and it is said that family worship, and the training up of their children in the ways of religion, are not generally attended to by professors.

METHODISTS.

The sentiments of this sect are well known; they are uniform in their opinions and discipline, throughout America, being all followers of Wesley, who professed himself to be an Arminian. The discipline of the Methodists in America does not materially differ from that of those in England. Their clergy are bishops, elders, and deacons. The bodies which transact the general concerns of the connection, are the general and annual conferences. The field of labor is divided into districts, circuits, and classes. Each circuit has one itinerant or more, whose business it is to visit and preach to the classes in his circuit every two or three weeks. Each district has a presiding elder who is to visit the circuits in the way stated above. The classes meet weekly, for prayer, singing, and relation of their progress in religion; and it is the business of the class leader to examine every one of the class, at this time, and rebuke, comfort, or exhort as the case of each may require. To be admitted a member of the class, all that is necessary is to express their desire, and they are admitted to the privileges of their church, without any appearance of holiness of heart. In order to be admitted as a preacher, a recommendation is required of the character and talents of the person, from the class to which he belongs. He is then admitted by the bishop on trial one year. If his conduct is approved at the expiration of the time, he is admitted into full connection; at the end of the second year, to the order of deacon, and the next year if approved, he is ordained an elder. These preachers, on trial, sometimes turn out very vile. In general, they have little learning; though when they begin to preach, they begin to study, and many of them improve considerably. As to their manner of preaching, it very much resembles that of the Baptists.—is very controversial, and most bitter against Calvinists. They rail very much against the practice of the Presbyterians' receiving pay for preaching, calling them hirelings, but most unreasonably; for their salaries are more certain, and, in general, greater than those against whom they speak. According to their discipline, each preacher, who itinerates, besides all his expenses, is to receive $ 80 for himself, $ 80 for his wife, and a certain sum for each of his children, according to their ages, and a support when worn out in the service. This denomination has greatly increased within a few years, and this must chiefly be attributed to their complete system of missions, which is by far the best for domestic missions ever yet adopted. They send their laborers into every corner of the country; if they hear of any particular attention to religion in a place, they double the number of laborers in those circuits, and place their best men there, and endeavor generally, to adapt the character of their preachers, to the character of the people among whom they are to labor.

NEW LIGHTS.

This sect arose in Kentucky in Sept. 1803, with five ministers of the Presbyterian church who were deposed by the Synod of Kentucky for teaching error. This people believed that the extraordinary work then existing in the western country was the beginning of the Millennium, and that all those doctrines which were hard to be understood, and that all mystery and obscurity in Scripture, would now be more clearly made known, so as to be understood and comprehended by every body. The first discovery which they pretended to make was, that all confessions of faith and catechisms were made by fallible men, erroneous, contrary to Scripture and reason, and calculated to keep believers in bondage. They therefore renounced them all, except the Bible. Next, that all Assemblies, Synods, and Presbyteries were contrary to Scripture, carnal bonds, and stood full in the way of Christ, and the revivals of religion; that the doctrine of divine decrees destroys free agency and makes men mere machines; that men were not justified by faith in Christ; that the doctrine of the Trinity leads to Tritheism; that Christ was not God, but man only, or at most a being of the highest order; that it was his duty to love and serve God with all his power, and he could therefore make no atonement for others; that there was no merit in his sufferings,

F

and in wrath in God which needed to be appeased, and therefore there was neither a necessity nor a possibility of his vicarious sufferings ; that the object of Christ's mission was to make atonement, reconciliation, &c. but that propitiation, reconciliation, and atonement mean the same thing, and that *atonement* being a word compounded of *at-one-ment*, signifies to make one, for *ment* is a Gaelic word signifying to make. But as God cannot change, the change must be in man, and atonement, therefore, means the same as repentance, or turning to God. This is a specimen of their criticism. They pretend to make discoveries, and to make plain many mysteries, to mention which, is unnecessary. I would only observe, that some made the discovery, that there would be no resurrection or future judgment. Thus it appears that a wild fanaticism in the West, has thrown nearly the same light on the Scriptures and religion, with which a boasted philosophy has illumined them in the East. This sect is without order, regularity, or any bond of union ; each does that which is right in his own eyes. They are as ignorant as any of the sects, and in their manner of preaching are much like those already noticed.—This denomination was once numerous, but they are dwindling away rapidly. Five or more of these preachers have made confessions and recantations, and are re-admitted to the Presbyterian church. Many have joined the Shakers, and probably the remainder will soon join the Baptists or Methodists.

HALCYONS.

The professed object of this sect is to effect a union between the several denominations professing faith in Christ, so as to eradicate all Sectarianism, and every party name out of the family of Jesus. They renounce all manner of creeds, confessions of faith, and catechisms hitherto published. They receive the holy Scriptures of the Old and New Testament as a sacred and divine help, handed from heaven to aid their reason in forming just ideas of the divine character and of divine things. But say they, "We receive not even the holy Scriptures as the foundation of our faith or religion, for we conceive that other foundation can never be laid, equal to the foundation stone which was laid before Joshua, (of which the Scriptures clearly speak,) whereon were seven eyes, which we conceive to be the seven communicable attributes of God.—*H. Epist. No.* 44. and 45. *Lex.* 1803. They consider Adam as a figure of Christ ; that the covenant made with him was a natural covenant, and deny that he could forfeit, even by transgression, the right and title of himself and offspring to eternal life and blessings ; in other words, forfeit any thing more than natural life, and natural blessings. The first office of Christ on earth was to explain the eternal laws of religion to man. They perform baptism by immersion or sprinkling, as the subject chooses, in the name of Jesus, by whom, they say, is exhibited in one glorious person, Father, Son, and Holy Ghost. They enter not into the state of matrimony, and look upon it as an ordinance of man, but choose spiritual mates. The whole of their scheme seems to be, to fill up the mystery of iniquity. Their leader was a man by all accounts, of vile character, who lately, it is reported, betrayed the confidence reposed in him, by a weak and half witted man, one of his own followers, that sent him to Philadelphia to receive a large sum of money for him, which this leader expended in the purchase of a large tract of land near the Sciota River, where he has invited all his followers to settle. This sect does not increase, and its number at present is small. The *Halcyon Luminary* published in New York, it is suppos'd, was conducted by some of this connection.

This report will be closed with a few observations on domestic missions. From the manner in which these are at present conducted, it is evident that but a small portion of the destitute parts of our country are visited by intelligent and correct missionaries ; and that many evils result, or at least that the good is not effected which might be, from the want of some regularly digested system, and co-operation of the different Missionary Societies, amongst Presbyterians and Congregationalists. It appears from the reports of the various Missionary Bodies, that the appointments of many of their missions are for a short time; from four to six, eight or ten weeks, seldom for six months or a year. Half of the time of these short appointments is sometimes taken up in going and returning from the field of labor. When they arrive there, they find the field so extensive, and their time so short, that they can stay only a day or two in a place, and then perhaps it is a year, or years before those places are visited again. Little or no good therefore can arise from such missionaries, in places as dissolute as we generally find our new settlements. It frequently happens, that different Missionary Bodies, from the want of understanding each other's appointments, send their missionaries to the same places, and therefore at times, two or three missionaries are found in the same region, while many of the most destitute places are entirely overlooked or neglected. But the great evil is, that the principal object of missions, (at least what the apostle of the Gentiles considered such, and to which he directed his efforts) the planting of churches, cannot receive attention. Some Missionary Societies, particularly the one of which you, Gentlemen, are the Trustees, have seen these difficulties, and have, in some measure, remedied them, by stationing missionaries at certain places, with directions to labor within a circumscribed region. To remedy another evil, there appears to be no provision, and that is, to prevent the good done from being frustrated or destroyed. The conclusion of a mission at the time when it begins to be useful, only opens a door for preachers of different denominations to creep in, and propagate their peculiar sentiments. On returning to such places after a year's absence, those whose attention was excited to divine things, are found to have joined the Baptists, Methodists, New Lights, or Halcyons.

Permit me to suggest to your Board, the ideas which occurred to me, while passing over the vast field for missions in the western States, respecting a plan of operation for domestic missions. The field of missions should be divided into circuits, and these into societies and places for preaching, so that a missionary by preaching three or four times in a week could visit each society once a month, or more frequently as circumstances should direct. That no missionary should be employed for less than one year; and that however small the number of circuits, there should be an immediate succession of laborers. That the great object should be to organize churches and societies, and thus prevent Sectaries from establishing themselves. That besides preaching, the business of the missionary should be to give catechetical instructions to the children; to distribute Tracts and Bibles; to organize social libraries, and societies for the suppression of vice: to search out young men of piety and talents, and encourage them to prepare for the ministry; and if poor, to urge it upon the people of his circuit, as a duty to contribute to their support, so that the churches which may be organized may raise up ministers for their own supply. The societies at the different places should be so organized as to meet every Sabbath, although they have no preaching, for the purpose of singing, prayer, and reading the Scriptures, sermons, or some religious intelligence. I have known a revival of religion to commence at such a meeting, in Ohio, on Buck Creek, Champaign county. It would perhaps be highly proper, as most of the missionaries on the circuit will probably be young men, to have as many experienced ministers as can visit annually, semi-annually, or quarterly, the different circuits, receive the reports of the missionaries, and see that every thing be conducted with decency, propriety, and order, and make reports to the Missionary Societies.

How or where to obtain the missionaries, or the means to carry such a plan into effect, is the greatest difficulty. The way to obtain missionaries most readily would be for ministers and churches strongly to recommend and urge it upon all, who prepare for the ministry, to spend one or two years as a missionary, in the new settlements. It would be beneficial to those who engage in it on account of the opportunity of becoming acquainted with men in the various walks of life, of obtaining a more extensive knowledge of the world, and much experience on many points of great utility, in preparing them for the arduous task of taking charge of a particular people. Many too are so enfeebled by a long course of study, that the active labor of a missionary would greatly improve their health, and invigorate them for future service. That it would be beneficial to the new settlements is self-evident; that it would prove so to the churches in the old settlements. I think cannot be doubted, if it is any advantage to have ministers over them of some experience, vigor, and activity. As to the means of supporting such missions, from enquiry I am satisfied, that in the new settlements there would be voluntary contributions, sufficient at least to pay one half of their yearly stipend. All which is respectfully submitted by,

Yours with due consideration,

JOHN F. SCHERMERHORN.

Andover, (Mass.) December 10, 1813.

NOTES.

1. THE topographical remarks on the country are introduced to give the Trustees an idea in what parts of the country population, in all probability, will most rapidly increase ; and of course where missionary services will be most wanted. When any district of country is called comparatively poor or light soil, is meant when compared with the first rate lands in the western States ; though, at the same time, it may be first rate, when compared with the soil of the eastern States.

2. By *Vacant Societies*, in the Tables, must not always be understood churches already organized ; but, in most places, only congregations, or places of preaching.

3. The population in the different Counties is taken from the census of 1810 ; the number of ministers, churches, and vacant societies of the Presbyterians, from the minutes of different Presbyteries, and from the information of ministers ; the number of Baptist preachers, &c. in general, from their printed Association minutes, and where these could not be procured, from the best information that Baptist ministers could give ; the number of circuits, itinerants, and members of society of the Methodists, from the printed minutes of their annual Conference in 1812, and from the assistance of a presiding elder of information in Tennessee.

MR. MILLS' STATEMENT.

—◦✦◦—

TO THE TRUSTEES OF THE MISSIONARY SOCIETY OF CONNECTICUT,

GENTLEMEN,

IN my last, I gave you an account of my travels and missionary labors, from the time I left Hartford, till I arrived at Marietta.

I left Marietta the 24th of October, 1812, and proceeded down the Ohio River. On the 25th (Sabbath) preached at Belprie, a New England settlement. Thence proceeded through Galliopolis to Chilicothe, where I arrived November 2d, preaching occasionally on the way ; and distributing the Constitution of the Ohio Bible Society. The prospect was favorable as it respects the increase of the funds of the Society ; at least as much so as could be expected. On the 7th came to Springfield, on the head waters of the Little Miami. Here I tarried two or three days, detained on account of the rain, and waiting for Mr. Schermerhorn, who left Marietta the same day that I did. He went up the Muskingum, and came on by Zanesville and Franklinton to Springfield, where he arrived the 10th. We proceeded on our way to Dayton, and put up with Dr. Welch, the Presbyterian minister residing in that place. From Dayton, I came to Lebanon, near the Little Miami, and thence to Cincinnati. Brother Schermerhorn went down the Big Miami by Franklin to Cincinnati, at which place we both arrived the 17th of November.

South of New Connecticut, few Bibles or religious tracts have been received for distribution among the inhabitants. The Sabbath is greatly profaned ; and but few good people can be found in any one place. There are, however, a number of societies which are wishing to obtain ministers for settlement, for a part of the time at least, more commonly for six months in the year. The New Light societies have been numerous in the western part of the State ; but are at present fast declining. The Baptists are somewhat numerous in certain parts of the State. But the Methodists, according to their own calculation, are far the most numerous religious denomination, in the State of Ohio, south of New Connecticut, which is, in my opinion, far the most desirable part of the State; certainly as respects the moral and religious habits of the people living there. They are far advanced above any portion of country, of equal extent and population, west of the mountains.

From Cincinnati Mr. Schermerhorn and myself went down the river Ohio to Laurenceburgh in the Indiana Territory. Left that place the 24th of November, crossed the Ohio into Kentucky, and came down the river about 50 miles; then again crossed over into Indiana, and came down some miles on that side of the river; then crossed back into Kentucky, and continued our course within 30 miles of the falls of the Ohio, preaching occasionally. We found the inhabitants in a very destitute state; very ignorant of the doctrines of the Gospel; and in many instances without Bibles, or any other religious books. The Methodist preachers pass through this country, in their circuits occasionally; but do very little, I fear, towards aiding the people in obtaining a true knowledge of the doctrines of the Bible. There are a number of good people in the Territory, who are anxious to have Presbyterian ministers amongst them. They likewise wish to be remembered by Bible and Religious Tract Societies.

Leaving the river, we proceeded on our way through Frankfort, an easterly course to Lexington, where we arrived Dec. 5th. We put up with Mr. Blythe, and soon became acquainted with a number of good people. During our stay at Lexington, we assisted in re-organizing the Constitution of the Bible Society, which had been instituted a year or two before; but on too restrictive principles. It had done but little towards advancing the great object for which it was established. The prospect was, when we left, that it would soon become much more extensively useful. Of 500 Bibles, which had been committed to our care, by the New York Bible Society, we directed 100 to be sent to the managers of the Kentucky Society, for distribution.

We left Lexington the 14th of December, and proceeded on our way to Nashville, in Tennessee, where we arrived the 28th. On the 29th rode to Franklin, 20 miles from Nashville, and put up with Mr. Blackburn. During our stay in this part of Tennessee, we consulted with a number of pious people, with regard to the expediency of forming a Bible Society. They decidedly favored the object. Mr. Blackburn thought there would not be time to collect the people, and form a Constitution during our stay. He engaged that he would exert himself in favor of the object, as did others, men of piety and influence. We left with him a copy of the Constitution of the Bible Society formed in the State of Ohio; and wrote to Mr. Robbins of Marietta, requesting him to send to Nashville, for the benefit of the Society about to be formed in that neighborhood, 50 of the 500 Bibles which were to be sent to him from Pittsburgh.

We consulted with Mr. Blackburn on the expediency of pursuing our course down the river to New Orleans. He advised us to go, and assisted in making the necessary preparations. It was thought best for us to descend the river. General Jackson was expecting to go in a few days, with about 1500 Volunteers to Natchez. Mr. Blackburn introduced us to the General, who, having become acquainted with our design, invited us to take passage on board his boat. We accepted the invitation; and after providing some necessary stores for the voyage, and making sale of our horses, we embarked the 10th of January, 1813. We came to the mouth of the Ohio the 27th, where we lay by three days on account of the ice. On the 31st we passed New Madrid; and the 16th of February arrived at Natchez.

During our stay at Natchez and the vicinity, we introduced the subject of the formation of a Bible Society, for the benefit of the destitute in the Missisippi Territory. The professedly religious people, of the different denominations, appeared anxious for the establishment of an Institution of this kind. A proposal was drawn up for a meeting of those disposed to aid the object and the time and place of the meeting agreed upon. At the time appointed, a number assembled, and chose a Committee to prepare a Constitution to be presented to those disposed to sign it, at a second meeting which was to be held at Natchez, three weeks from the first meeting. We left with the Committee a copy of the Constitution we had with us, to which the one formed for the Missisippi Territory will most likely be similar. The Bible Society for this Territory will be supported by a number of the most influential characters, both civil and religious. W engaged to send them 100 Bibles, and have given directions that they should be forwarded to Natchez. We likewise encouraged them to hope for further donations of Bibles from other Societies; and engaged, upon our return, to represent their state to the Bible Societies of Philadelphia, Connecticut, and Massachusetts. As those who engaged in the formation of the Society, entered upon the subject in a very spirited manner, we doubt not the result will be a happy one.

Before we left Natchez, we (with Mr. Blackman, the chaplain who attended the Tennessee Volunteers) obtained a subscription of more than $ 100 for the benefit of the Tennessee Bible Society. This subscription was made by the officers principally. The prospect was that it would be very considerably increased, before they left that part of the country. We were treated with great attention by the General and Officers; and were more obliged to them for their subscription to the Tennessee Society, than if it had been made to us.

We left Natchez the 12th of March, and went on board a flat bottomed boat, where our accommodations were but indifferent. The weather was generally pleasant, and we arrived at New

G

Orleans the 19th. We might have taken passage in the steam boat, and should have done so, had it not been for the extra expense we must have incurred. The usual rate each passenger pays in the steam boat from Natchez to New Orleans is $ 18; whereas our passage was but little more than $ 6 for both of us. The distance is 300 miles. For 100 miles above New Orleans, the banks of the river are cleared, and in descending the river you pass many very elegant plantations. The whole of this distance, the banks appear like one continued village. The greater part of the inhabitants are French Catholics, ignorant of almost every thing except what relates to the increase of their property; destitute of Schools, Bibles, and religious instruction. In attempting to learn the religious state of these people, we were frequently told, that they had no Bibles, and that the priests did not allow of their distribution among them. An American, who had resided two or three years at a place, which has the appearance of being a flourishing settlement, and which has a Chatholic church, informed me that he had not seen a Bible during his stay at the settlement. He added, that he had heard that a woman from the State of New York had lately brought one into the place.

Upon our arrival at New Orleans, we were soon made acquainted with a few religious people. The number of those possessing this character, in this place, we are constrained to believe is small. We found here a Baptist minister, who has been in the city a few months, but expects to leave the place soon He is a sensible man, and to appearance a Christian. I doubt not, he has labored faithfully in the service of his Master There is no Protestant church in the city. Attempts have been made to obtain a subscription for building one, but have failed. There is at present a Methodist preacher in the place. I believe he expects to leave it soon. The Catholic priests will then be the only professedly religious teachers in the city.

Soon after our arrival, we introduced the subject of a Bible Society. It directly met the wishes of the religious people with whom we had become acquainted. As we had letters of introduction to Governor Clairborne, we called upon him in company with a friend. The object of our coming to the place was stated to him, and he approved of it. A proposal for a meeting was readily signed by him, and by 12 of the members of the Legislature who were then in session. About 20 more, principally merchants belonging to the city, added their names to the list. At the time appointed for establishing a Society, the greater part of those who subscribed to the proposal met. Previous to the meeting, a Constitution had been formed; and was presented for their approbation, should it meet the wishes of those present. The Constitution was read and considered, article by article, and adopted. It provided that the number of Managers should not be less than 12, nor more than 24. The Managers were to choose the other officers of the

Society. After signing the Constitution, the Managers were chosen, about 20, some residing in the country, but the greater part in the city. The Managers proceeded to the choice of officers. General Benjamin Morgan was chosen President, and Dr. Dow, Vice-President. The rate paid by those who become members is fixed at $ 5, upon signing the paper, and the yearly tax upon each member is $ 3. All present appeared much gratified with the opening prospect.

We found that, in order to have the Bible circulate freely, especially among the Catholics, the consent of those high in office must be obtained. We were frequently told, that the Catholic priests would by no means favor the object. We were referred to Father Antonio, as he is called, who has greater influence with those of his order than even the Bishop, who has lately arrived from Baltimore. If the consent of the former could be obtained, it was allowed by those with whom we conversed, that much might be done towards distributing the Scriptures among the French Catholics. We took a convenient opportunity to call upon the Reverend Father. The subject was mentioned to him. He said he should be pleased to have the Bible circulate among those of his order ; and that he would approve of the translation distributed by the *British and Foreign Bible Society.* In addition to this, he said he would aid in the circulation of the Scriptures should an opportunity present. We enquired of him, whether the priests in the different parishes would likewise favor the good work ? At this enquiry he seemed surprised, and answered, " How can you doubt it ? It is for their interest to circulate the Scriptures." Upon this point, our sentiments were hardly in unison. However we felt no disposition to contradict him. We have since called upon the Bishop. He also gave his consent, and said he would contribute in favor of the infant Institution. This disposition in the Catholic priests to favor the circulation of the Scriptures has very much surprised all with whom we have conversed on the subject in the city. The priests acknowledge the nakedness of the land. Father Antonio gave it as his opinion, that we should very rarely find a Bible in any of the French or Spanish Catholic families, in any of the parishes. And the Bishop remarked, that he did not believe there were 10 Bibles in the possession of all the Catholic families in the State ; and these families constitute three-fourths of the population of the State, people of color excepted, as is believed by men of information. When we came to this place, we found a number of French Bibles and Testaments had been sent here for distribution, gratis ; and had been on hand some time. They are now all disposed of, and repeated enquiries are made for those books by the Catholics. I happened in at Mr. Stackhouse's store a short time since. During my stay, which was short, five or six persons came in, enquiring for the Bible in the French language. The present is certainly a new and interesting æra in the history of New Orleans. Mr. Stackhouse informs me, that if he had 50 Bibles, he could dispose of them at once to the Catholics.

We expect to leave this place soon, and proceed on our way to Georgia, through the Creek nation. We hope to arrive home early in the month of July.

Yours very respectfully,

SAMUEL J. MILLS.

New Orleans, April 3, 1813.

NOTE.

Those parts of Mr. Mills' letter are omitted which contain a statement of the number of ministers, churches, &c. of various denomination, because that number is particularly detailed in Mr. Schermerhorn's letter, and it was thought unnecessary to publish the same thing twice over.

REPORT

OF A

MISSIONARY TOUR

THROUGH THAT PART OF THE UNITED STATES

WHICH LIES WEST OF

THE ALLEGANY MOUNTAINS;

PERFORMED UNDER THE DIRECTION

OF THE

MASSACHUSETTS MISSIONARY SOCIETY.

BY SAMUEL J. MILLS AND DANIEL SMITH.

ANDOVER:

PRINTED BY FLAGG AND GOULD.

1815.

ADVERTISEMENT.

DURING the years 1812 and 1813, the Rev. Messrs. Schermerhorn and Mills performed a Missionary Tour through most of the United States. They were guided by instructions received from the Trustees of certain Missionary Societies in New England. The principal objects of their Mission were—to preach the gospel to the destitute, —to explore the country and learn its moral and religious state,—and to promote the establishment of Bible Societies, and of other religious and charitable institutions. The friends of religion, who are desirous to learn what were the exertions and success of the Missionaries, are referred to their printed Reports, designated as follows :—

" A correct view of that part of the United States, which lies west of the Allegany mountains, with regard to religion and morals. By John F. Schermerhorn and Samuel J. Mills." Printed at Hartford, Con. 1814.

" Report to the Society for propagating the Gospel among the Indians and others in North America."

" Communications relative to the progress of Bible Societies in the United States," addressed to the Bible Society of Philadelphia. Printed in Philadelphia, 1813. Reprinted at Baltimore.

In the years 1814 and 1815, Messrs. Mills and Smith performed a similar Missionary Tour, having the same objects, with some others, in view. An account of their exertions and success is presented to the public in the following Report.

CONTENTS.

———

REPORT.

—

I. INTRODUCTORY LETTER FROM MR. MILLS.

PITTSBURGH, PENN. AUG. 30, 1814.

*To the Committee appointed by the Trustees of the Massachusetts Mis-
sionary Society, to superintend a mission to the western and south-
western parts of the United States:*

GENTLEMEN,

I received your Instructions, dated the 7th of July last, previously
to my leaving Boston. In the instructions, you advised me to proceed to Connecticut, and make arrangements for the then contemplated mission. A proper companion to accompany me on the mission,
had not at that time been obtained. In compliance with your instructions, I went on to Connecticut, and engaged as my fellow labourer
Mr. Daniel Smith. As Mr. Smith was known to you, and as we had
previously conversed together respecting his qualifications for the
mission, and found our sentiments to be in unison, I did not hesitate
to engage him to accompany me.*

Together with your instructions, I received from you a Statement,
presenting your views of the importance of the mission, addressed
" To the friends of religion in general: but particularly, to the Directors and Trustees of the Connecticut Missionary Society, the Connecticut Bible Society, the New-York Bible Society, the New-York
Missionary Society, and the Philadelphia Bible Society." The object of this Statement was (as you will recollect) to give an opportunity to the Trustees and Directors of the above-named charitable
associations, to aid in defraying the expenses incurred by the missionaries, and also to make up to them a reasonable compensation for
their services.

Agreeably to your instructions, the Statement was presented to the
Directors and Trustees of the several Societies to whom it was addressed. But we did not receive any promise of support from any of
them, until we arrived at Philadelphia. The Managers of the Bible
Society of that place, had previously given encouragement, that they
would make a considerable donation in our favour, on condition, that

* That Mr. Smith was approved by you, we had full confirmation from your letter dated Aug. 24, and received by us at Marietta, Sept. 10.

we would take charge of an edition of French New Testaments, designed for gratuitous distribution, among the Roman Catholics, in the western and southern portions of our country. Before we left Philadelphia, they concluded that they would secure to us six hundred dollars.*

Your Statement was also presented, to the Trustees of the Philadelphia Missionary Society. Although their funds were small; and they had never before supported missionary exertions, except in the city and the vicinity; still they readily engaged to consider us as labouring in their service, one month each, while employed on the mission. The compensation they secured to us, for this service was one hundred dollars.

The whole amount of donations in support of the mission, when we left Philadelphia, was thirteen hundred dollars.

From the Massachusetts Missionary Society	$600
From the Philadelphia Bible Society	600
From the Philadelphia Missionary Society	100
	1300

Before we left Philadelphia, six hundred English Bibles were sent on to Pittsburgh. These Bibles were the donation of the Massachusetts Bible Society, committed to our care for distribution in the western country.—One hundred Bibles were forwarded to the care of Dr. Coffin, East Tennessee, for distribution. This donation was from the Female Missionary Society of Boston. About five thousand copies of the French New Testaments were also sent on to Pittsburgh. We received general instructions from the Managers of the Philadelphia Bible Society respecting the distribution of them. We had likewise at our disposal, about fifteen thousand Religious Tracts; published by the New England Tract Society, and committed to our care for distribution by a number of the original subscribers. In addition to the Tracts, we had a large quantity of Sermons and Pamphlets on a variety of religious subjects, principally donations from gentlemen residing in Massachusetts and Connecticut. We had also at our disposal, fifty copies of the Memoirs of Mrs. Harriet Newell. We had previously provided ourselves with a light waggon, which we proposed to retain as long as the roads in the new country would permit.

Thus equipt and followed by the prayers of many of the friends of Zion, we left Philadelphia on the 15th inst. and proceeded on our way to this place. We arrived on the 28th.

In the interiour of this State, there are extensive tracts of country very destitute of religious privileges; especially the vallies between the Allegany mountains. The inhabitants of these vallies have as yet been in a great measure neglected by Missionary Societies. Very little exertion has been made, to supply the destitute with Bibles and religious books. We distributed among them a considerable quantity

* This Society had printed 5000 copies of the French New Testament, for gratuitous distribution; and 1000 of superior execution for sale. 400 of these were entrusted to our care, to be disposed of for the benefit of the Society:—and they were afterwards purchased by the Bible Society of Louisiana, at 400 dollars.

of Tracts and Sermons. Their curiosity was excited, and in some instances the pamphlets were eagerly sought after. From what we could learn with respect to these people, we should be led to fear, that they are becoming more ignorant and vicious, as the settlements advance in age.

Yours with sentiments of esteem and affection,

SAMUEL J. MILLS.

Rev. SAMUEL WORCESTER, D. D.
JEREMIAH EVARTS, Esq.
HENRY GRAY, Esq.

II. *Exertions in favour of Bible Societies &c. north of the Ohio River.—Letters from Messrs. Mills and Smith.*

Somerset, Ohio, Sept. 21, 1814.

To the Rev. SAMUEL WORCESTER, D. D.

Dear Sir,

Mr. Evarts's letter of 24th ult. was received a few days since at Marietta. A storm that prevents our travelling, gives us time to acknowledge the receipt of it, and to report to you the progress we have been enabled to make in our mission. We left Philadelphia on the 15th of August and reached Pittsburgh on the 28th. There we tarried a few days waiting the arrival of the Bibles and Tracts committed to our care; which we had reason to expect would have been there sooner than ourselves. But as we could not be long detained, we left orders for them to be forwarded to Marietta, and went on our way. Mr. Mills went through Steubenville to Wheeling, (Vir.) and Mr. Smith through Cannonsburgh and Washington. At Cannonsburgh there is a college, which has been a great blessing to that portion of the country. Most of the clergy have been educated at it. The Rev. Mr. Wiley is the principal. He is assisted by two others. The present number of students is about forty. There is a fund here for the education of pious young men for the ministry, capable of supporting a small number. At Washington, 6 miles off, there is another college. The Rev. Mr. Brown is the principal. There are about sixty students. At Washington, Mr. Smith was present at a meeting for the formation of a Bible Society, and assisted in its organization. It was a pleasant meeting. A number of clergymen and others, of different religious denominations, were present. The business was entered upon with unanimity and with engagedness. The Society is denominated " *The Bible Society at Washington, (Penn.)*" The Rev. John Anderson, is the President. About twenty persons subscribed the constitution. There is a prospect of 150 or 200 members.* The people of the western parts of Pennsylvania, are perhaps more highly

* The Bible Society at Washington Penn. as we have lately learnt, is very flourishing. It is established in a new country and confined to a small district : There is another older Society at Pittsburgh. Yet this infant institution has received funds to the amount of five hundred dollars. It has a country deplorably destitute of the Scriptures, in its immediate vicinity, in the borders of Virginia—and has begun a career of benevolent exertion, that will only end, we are confident, with the universal diffusion of religious knowledge.

favoured with respect to religious privileges than any other portion of the western country. And they appear to prize their privileges. Mr. Smith attended a sacrament at Wheeling, which is near the borders of Pennsylvania, and saw females of respectable appearance walking four or five miles to meeting. The Lord we hope is about to excite this people to exert themselves in extending these privileges to their destitute neighbours and brethren.

We met at Grave Creek, having been separated for several days. As we were travelling on the banks of the Ohio, we were forcibly impressed with the idea, that a mission ought, if possible, to be speedily established on the banks of this river. Permit us, dear Sir, through you, to urge this station upon the notice of your Society; and perhaps of other Missionary Societies in New England. Between Steubenville and Marietta, (a distance of about a hundred miles,) there is no regular clergyman. Only one place, Wheeling, is supplied with Presbyterian preaching half the time. This ground seems also to be very much deserted by Baptists and Methodists. There might be, on both sides of the river, as many as eight or ten stations selected, where very considerable congregations might be convened to hear the Gospel preached. These stations might be visited by a missionary once in a fortnight or three weeks: and in this way, as many people would be supplied with the Gospel, as perhaps could be supplied by the same trouble and expense, in any other portion of our new country. The people on this station, so far as we could learn, appear to be willing to attend meeting. At Grave Creek, Mr. Mills appointed a lecture; and in about two hours more than fifty people came together. A missionary on this station, might have frequent opportunities of exerting a salutary influence upon the boatmen that navigate the river; who are a set of men as much corrupted perhaps, as any in the country. The distribution of Bibles and Religious Tracts, both among the boatmen and the inhabitants, would be a very pleasant and promising part of his business. The river bottom, extending one or two miles in width, is extremely fertile, and will no doubt in a few years have a very numerous population. To preoccupy this field is a matter of immense importance to the interests of the Redeemer's kingdom in this vicinity.

We arrived at Marietta on the 8th inst. On our inquiring into the state of the Ohio Bible Society, we were happy to learn, that it appears to be flourishing, and bids fair to be a powerful instrument in diffusing the knowledge of the Scriptures throughout the western world. This Society was formed about two years since, when Messrs. Mills and Schermerhorn were at Marietta on their former mission.

During the first year after its formation, the Society received from subscribers nearly two hundred dollars. Since the commencement of the present year it has received nearly four hundred dollars. This Society has received from the Massachusetts Bible Society a donation of one hundred dollars; from the Connecticut Bible Society three donations amounting to five hundred Bibles; from the New York Bible Society a donation of one hundred Bibles; and from the Philadelphia Bible Society a donation of thirty-one Bibles and sixty-eight Testaments. The Society has actually distributed four hundred and eighty one Bibles and sixty-seven Testaments, and has now sent to Philadelphia to purchase four hundred Bibles more.

This Society has also, apparently, been the means of *provoking to emulation* the good people in other parts of the State. A Bible Society has been formed in the Connecticut Reserve, which has already sent to Philadelphia for six hundred Bibles. Another is formed at Chillicothe; and another is contemplated at Cincinnati. Measures are now taking to unite these several Societies, and others that may be formed, into one general State Society. While we tarried at Marietta, our Bibles and Tracts arrived. We repacked them as soon as possible, and ordered them to different places, still farther to the west and south. We are now again on our journey. Whether we shall be able to penetrate as far west as St. Louis, we know not. It is apprehended to be dangerous travelling through the Territories, on account of hostile Indians. May the Lord direct us in the path of duty, and be our Protector; then we shall be safe.

Hitherto the Lord has wonderfully preserved us. We can say with truth, that on our long journey no harm worth mentioning has been suffered to befal us. Why then should we now distrust the providence of God? We proceed therefore with confidence, followed, we hope, by many prayers.

We are, dear Sir, yours most affectionately, &c.

III. *Exertions in favour of Bible Societies continued.*

St. Louis, Missouri Territory, Nov. 7, 1814.

Dear Sir,—Our last communication to you was dated, near Lancaster, Ohio, Sept. 21. We have delayed writing to you, longer than we otherwise should, because our plans of conduct have hitherto been somewhat undetermined. We did not know, that we should be able to reach this place. But through the kind providence and protection of our God, we have passed safely through the wilderness, and have now reached the most western point of our contemplated tour.

At Lancaster, we called on the Rev. Mr. Wright, a presbyterian clergyman. He has formerly been a laborious missionary; and has much information respecting the religious state of the western country. Since his settlement in that place, and within six years, he has distributed four hundred Bibles. He is therefore well acquainted with the proportionate number of the destitute, in Ohio. And, in his opinion, as many families, as one in five, are not possessed of the Scriptures. According to this estimate, more than *thirteen thousand* Bibles are necessary, in order that there may be one to each family. Here is a large field for the exercise of Christian liberality. Mr. Wright relates some signal instances of the blessed effects of giving away the Bible. He has seen a man notorious for indifference to religion, and for profaneness, suddenly arrested in his career of stupidity and folly, by this simple means. He has seen him turned about, and in the judgment of charity thoroughly converted from the error of his ways, and made a humble worshipper of the Lord Jesus. And all this was effected by *the gift of a Bible.* What Christian—what friend of humanity, would not give *sixty cents* to bring about an event like this !*

From Lancaster we proceeded to Chillicothe; tarried there a day or two, and went on to Cincinnati.—The presbytery in that vicinity, had been for some time endeavouring to procure the formation of a Bible Society for the country between the Miamies. But they had not effected it. We suggested to a number of clergymen, who were providentially in town, the expediency of proceeding immediately to the formation of a Society. They approved of the proposal, and gave notice of a meeting for the purpose. The next day we had the satisfaction of seeing a number of clergymen and others, of different denominations, assembled. But as many were not present, whose assistance was desired, it was thought best to postpone the matter until the next week. A committee was appointed to prepare a constitution, and notice was given of another meeting.—Cincinnati contains 5,000 inhabitants, and has a rich back country. We doubt not, therefore, that before this time a Society is formed there, which will be a powerful instrument, in the diffusion of the Sacred Scriptures.† The ladies there have taken the precedency in that labour of love. They have associated themselves under the denomination of, " *The Female Society of Cincinnati for charitable purposes.*" They were about to send to the managers of the Ohio Bible Society, to procure for them one hundred Bibles. Agreeably to your instructions, we made known to the Rev. Mr. Wilson the circumstances of the mission with respect to support; and, at his request, after an evening service in which Mr. Mills preached, a contribution was received in aid of the mission. It amounted to twenty dollars—to which the Ladies' Society added twenty dollars more. Of these, and other similar donations, a strict account will be given to your Society. At Cincinnati we submitted the question to the decision of a number of Presbyterian clergymen, whether we ought to attempt to go through the western Territories to this place. They unanimously decided that we ought to go forward. We therefore went on: But we did it with some degree of hesitancy. For we were obliged, in a great measure, to relinquish a promising field of usefulness in the neighbourhood of Cincinnati, and also in the neighbourhood of Lexington, (Ken.)

As we passed through the Indiana Territory, we kept steadily in view the great object of procuring the formation of a Bible Society there. We conversed with gentlemen of the first respectability from Lawrenceburgh to Vincennes. And although some had never even heard of such an institution; yet all without exception approved of the object. We had several interviews with Governor Posey at Jeffersonville. He gave his decided approbation; and said he would

---

* See Appendix, A.

† At the time appointed, a Bible Society was organized at Cincinnati, for the country between the Miamies, and obtained subscriptions to the amount of three hundred dollars. When we received our last information from that place, subscription papers had been printed and circulated; and funds had been obtained to a much larger amount. Exertions were still making to increase the amount of the Society's resources.

exert himself in favour of such a Society. The population of this Territory is increasing with surprising rapidity. In 1810 it amounted to little more than 24,000. Now it is thought there are 50,000 inhabitants. Very many of these are poor people, and destitute of the Scriptures.

In the Illinois Territory, we pursued the same course; and were so happy as to meet with universal countenance and approbation. At Shawanee-town we saw Judge Griswold, formerly from Connecticut. He will be a decided friend of the Bible Society. He favoured us with letters of introduction to Governor Edwards, and other gentlemen at Kaskaskias. The Governor has promised to patronize the Society should one be formed. This Territory is deplorably destitute of Bibles. In Kaskaskias, a place containing from 80 to 100 families, there are, it is thought, not more than four or five. At *Prairie du Rocher* we had an interesting conversation with Bishop Flaget of the Roman Catholic church, respecting the distribution of the sacred volume among his people. He said he heartily approved; and would exert himself to promote the circulation of the French Scriptures among the Catholics of his diocese:—with only this reserve, that he must first examine the translation, and see that it is one approved by the church.

In this Territory, our prospects are flattering with respect to the formation of a Bible Society. The measure has many friends;—we have yet heard of none who oppose it. Governor Clark has already become a subscriber. We have strong hopes, therefore, that we shall soon see respectable Bible Societies established in each of the Territories. Such institutions are certainly very much needed. It is exceedingly difficult, even for those who have money, to procure Bibles. Very few are ever offered for sale. Many of the inhabitants are unable to buy. The Methodist church sends very considerable quantities of other books into this country for sale; but it sends no Bibles— or almost none.* We have much regretted, in passing through the Territories, that we were not able to proceed more slowly, and to perform more *missionary labour*. But considering the length of our tour, and the advanced season of the year, we have done what we could. Sure we are, that no person, who has one spark of benevolence in his heart, can forbear to exert himself, while passing through this land of darkness and the shadow of death.

From this place we expect to return immediately, through Illinois and Indiana, to Louisville and Lexington, Kentucky; and then to proceed, as expeditiously as circumstances will permit, to Natchez, and New Orleans.

Yours in the bonds of Christian affection.

IV. *Exertions in favour of Bible Societies continued.*

Shawanee-town, Illinois Territory, Jan. 12, 1815.
To JEREMIAH EVARTS, *Esq.*
Dear Sir,—We wrote our last letter to Dr. Worcester, from St. Louis, in the early part of November. Since that date, we have, with

* See Appendix, B.

the blessing of God upon our exertions, completed a prosperous tour through the Territories, Indiana, Illinois, and Missouri. In our former letter we gave you a brief view of our exertions in favour of the formation of Bible Societies for the Territories, until the date of our letter. Previous to our leaving St. Louis, a subscription paper was circulated in order to ascertain who would favour the formation of a Bible Society for the Territory. Near three hundred dollars were subscribed in the course of a day or two, by the inhabitants of that place. The subscribers engaged to pay the sums annexed to their names, to the proper officer of their Society, when it should be organized. There was a meeting of a number of the subscribers. They chose a committee to draw up the Constitution of a Bible Society, and appoint a second meeting, when they proposed to adopt it. Before we left the Territory, a subscription paper to aid the object of the contemplated Bible Society was drawn up at the lead mines, and another at St. Genevieve. We have not as yet ascertained the amount subscribed at these places. From the disposition manifested, by a number of influential characters in these two places, we doubt not considerable sums will be subscribed. We ascertained, that there never had been any English Bibles, or French Testaments, sent into this Territory for gratuitous distribution, except in one instance. Some time since, the Directing Committee of the Bible Society of Philadelphia sent to the care of Dr. Elliot, then residing at St. Genevieve, a number of English Bibles and French Testaments to be distributed by him. The English Bibles were very soon given out, and the French Testaments principally.* This Territory presents a very important and interesting field for missionary labours. There are many persons here, who have heretofore been members, either of Congregational or Presbyterian churches; and who regret, with many a heart-ache, and many a tear, the loss of former privileges, and are looking with anxiety toward the rising sun, for some one to come to them, who shall stand and feed them in the name of Christ, and break to them the bread of life.

November 9th, we left St. Louis, crossed the Mississippi, and proceeded on our way to Kaskaskias. Previously to our leaving Kaskaskias, we had a second conversation with Governor Edwards on the subject of the proposed Bible Society in the Illinois Territory. He expressed his earnest desire, that the Society might soon go into operation. He was anxious that we should stay until it was organized; but as it would be a considerable time before the notice of the meeting could be extensively circulated, we did not think it proper to delay. We had previously conversed with some of the most influen-

* A letter from Mr. Stephen Hempsted of St. Ferdinand, near St. Louis dated March 27, 1815, mentions, that the exertions, that have been made to procure the formation of a Bible Society for the Missouri Territory, have met with some opposition, so that the institution contemplated has not yet been organized. But the measure has many friends, who still keep the object in view. Among whom is Governor Clark and many of the most respectable inhabitants of the Territory. Among a thousand good ends, that would be answered by stationing a missionary in this Territory, one would be, the permanent establishment of this institution, that is now struggling into existence.

tial characters, of the different denominations, upon the subject of forming the Society. They not only approved of the Society, but engaged that they would exert themselves in favour of its formation. We did not find any place in this Territory, where a copy of the Scriptures could be obtained. Merchants occasionally bring into the Territories books of this description. The common school Bible is not unfrequently sold for two dollars. When we consider the inferior manner in which the Bible is often printed, this is certainly a very high price.

On the 14th of November we left Kaskaskias, and proceeded on our way to Shawanee-town. On our return to this place Judge Griswold informed us, that exertions were making to form a Bible Society for the eastern part of the Illinois Territory. He thought it most likely these exertions would prove successful.*

We could not ascertain, that there had ever been any Bibles or Testaments sent into this Territory for gratuitous distribution, and comparatively but a few families are supplied with either. Some, who are anxious to obtain the Bible, and able to purchase it, have been for years destitute. One man, whom we saw in this Territory, informed us, that for ten or fifteen years he had been using exertions to obtain the Sacred Scriptures, but without success.† Notwithstanding there are many ready and able to purchase the Scriptures, still there are many others who cannot with convenience supply themselves; and must for years, perhaps as long as they live, be destitute of the Bible in their families, unless their wants are relieved by others who have ability and a disposition to supply them.

We arrived at Vincennes, on the 19th of November. While we were at that place, a subscription paper was circulated, similar to the one circulated at St. Louis. One hundred dollars were very soon subscribed. The prospect was, that twice that sum would soon be obtained. The subscribers appointed a second meeting, when they proposed to adopt the constitution of a Bible Society for the western part of the Indiana Territory, or rather the Wabash District.‡ On the 25th of November, we arrived at New Albany, near Jeffersonville, which is situated at the falls of the Ohio. While we remained in the vicinity of the falls, subscription papers were circulated to ascertain who would aid the proposed Bible Society for the eastern part of the territory. These papers were circulated in Jeffersonville, New Albany, and Charlestown. Near 250 dollars were soon subscribed; and a time was appointed for the meeting, when it was expected the constitution would be adopted.§

* A day or two after this letter was written, we arrived at Shawanee-town, on our passage down the river, Judge Griswold informed us that nothing but the prevalence of a severe epidemick had prevented the formation of a Bible Society, on Christmas day, the time appointed for that purpose. He said the object was kept steadily in view, and he did not doubt but it would shortly be effected. Other gentlemen expressed the same opinion.—Judge G. had received the box of fifty Bibles which we had forwarded to his care. Already had there been many more applications for them than could be supplied.

† See Appendix, C.   ‡ For the result of these exertions, See Appendix, D.
§ See Appendix, E.

More than 700 dollars have been subscribed, since we came into the Territories, to purchase Bibles to give to the destitute. We have no doubt that these subscriptions will be very considerably increased. But a few of the people, disposed to favour the object, have had an opportunity to subscribe. Papers will be more generally circulated, when the societies shall go into operation. Some parts of the Territories are settling very fast. Many poor people are among the number of those, who go north of the Ohio. If those good men, who are disposed to favour the promotion of religion and morality, by the general distribution of the Sacred Scriptures among the destitute, continue to exert themselves, as we believe they will, still resources cannot be collected probably by them, more than sufficient to supply the yearly increasing destitute part of their population. From the best estimate, we could make, with respect to the proportionate number of destitute families in the three territories, we are led to believe, that 10 or 12,000 Bibles are necessary, in order to supply each destitute family.

You will readily perceive, Sir, that living as most of the people in the Territories do, 1000 or 1500 miles from any place where the Bible is printed, very many of them must for a long time remain destitute, unless their necessities can be relieved, at least in a considerable degree, by the Managers of Bible Societies in the different States. From the 600 Bibles committed to our care by the Committee of the Massachusetts Bible Society, 75 were ordered to the care of certain gentlemen in the Indiana Territory; 50 to Shawanee-town, to be distributed in the Illinois Territory; and 50 to St. Louis, to the care of Stephen Hempsted. Do, Sir, intercede with the managers of Bible Societies in your vicinity to aid in supplying the destitute poor in this portion of our country. The early part of December, we visited Lexington and Frankfort. Each of us at Frankfort had an opportunity of preaching to a number of the members of the Legislature, and of presenting them with a view of the object of our mission.

The 20th of December we returned to the Falls of the Ohio. We were detained at that place some time, waiting for a passage down the river to Natchez.

January 5th, we left Louisville, and embarked on board a keel-boat, descending the river to Natchez.—We lately received a letter from Mr. Hennen of New Orleans. He expressed his great satisfaction that the French Testaments were on their way to that place. He remarked in his letter, that the French people were frequently inquiring for them. He did not apprehend that any serious opposition would be made to their circulation from any quarter. Since we left Cincinnati, (Ohio,) we have followed the advice contained in your letter, relative to presenting the object of the mission, where we had a convenient opportunity, and receiving donations to aid in defraying the expenses. The result has been favourable. Near 300 dollars have been given to us for this purpose.

Thus far the Lord has prospered us, greatly prospered us. Dear Sir, pray for us, that God would still more abundantly succeed our feeble exertions to extend the kingdom of his Son; and may He grant that the dark valley of the Mississippi may soon be illuminated with the light of the everlasting Gospel.

V. *View of the country north of the Ohio, considered as a missionary field.*

On the *Mississippi, below New Madrid, Jan.* 20, 1815.

Rev. SAMUEL WORCESTER, D. D.

Dear Sir,—In our former letters we have detailed many of the interesting events of our mission. And we have occasionally hinted at *the importance of certain fields of missionary labour*, in the portions of country through which we have passed. We now beg leave to state, a little more at large, the observations we have made, and the thoughts that have occurred to us, on this interesting subject. We have already taken occasion to urge upon your notice, and the notice of your Society, a missionary circuit on the banks of the Ohio, between Steubenville and Marietta. We still think *that* a very important field, and should heartily rejoice to see it occupied by a faithful labourer. In the state of Ohio, other circuits, perhaps of equal importance, might be pointed out. But this has been already done by Mr. Schermerhorn. (See his " Correct View," &c.) This State, although in many parts deplorably destitute of the means of grace, is on the whole far better supplied both with established preachers and missionaries, than any of the States or Territories west or south of it. With a population of about 250,000; it has more than 50 Presbyterian and Congregational ministers—making an average of one preacher to 5000 inhabitants; while the State of Kentucky has not one Presbyterian minister to 10,000 inhabitants, and the North-western Territories not one to every 20,000. Ohio is fast emerging from the feeble, helpless state of infancy. Religion is taking deep root; and its branches are spreading from the river to the lake. Charitable institutions are formed and forming in various parts; such as Bible, Tract, and Moral Societies: and their salutary influence is beginning to be felt. But in other portions of western country it is not so. We propose, therefore, in this and some following communications to turn your attention more particularly to them. We begin with the Territories. We have travelled through them—have seen the nakedness of the land, and our eyes have affected our hearts. We have heard the cry, *Come over and help us.*

INDIANA, notwithstanding the war, is peopling very fast. Its settlements are bursting forth on the right hand and on the left. In 1810 there were in this Territory 24,500 inhabitants;—now they are computed by the Governor at 35,000 by others at 40, and by some at 50,000. Its principal settlements are on the Miami and Whitewater, —on the Ohio (extending in some places 20 miles back) and on the Wabash and White river. Many small neighbourhoods have received an addition of from 20 to 40 families during the last summer.

When we entered this Territory there was but one Presbyterian clergyman in it;—Mr. Scott of Vincennes. He has valiantly maintained his post there, for six years past. He has three places of preaching: and although he has not been favored with an extensive revival; yet his labors have been blest to the edification of his congregations. His church consists of about 70 members. Between the forks of White river, there is also a Presbyterian congregation; in which there are about 30 communicants:—and we have lately heard that a clergyman is now settled among them. In the State of Ohio we saw the Rev. William Robinson. He informed us, that he expected soon to remove to the Territory and establish himself at Madison on the Ohio. It is probable, then, that there are three Presbyterian clergymen now in the Territory. But what are they for the supply of so many thousands? They are obliged to provide principally for their own support, by keeping school through the week, or by manual labor. They have, therefore, very little time to itinerate. The settlements on the Miami and White-water, we did not visit; but were informed by Missionaries, who have occasionally laboured there, that they afford promising fields of usefulness. Probably congregations might be formed there. Places of preaching, where considerable numbers of people would assemble, might be established, with short intervals, from Lawrenceburgh, near the mouth of the Miami, to Jeffersonville, on the Falls of the Ohio. In the vicinity of the Falls, are two other flourishing little villages, Charlestown and New Albany. It is of high importance that the standard of the truth should be immediately planted here;—for these places, or some of them, must soon become rich and populous tows. At Charlestown, there is a small Presbyterian church. But it languishes for want of the bread and of the water of life. Leaving the river, and proceeding a little further west, we came to other flourishing settlements. Corydon is the present seat of government for the Territory. Salem, a county seat, has near it three other places where churches might be formed. These settlements are yet in there infancy. It is said, however, that they are able to support a minister. And yet there are people here, who, for five years past, have not seen the face of a Presbyterian clergyman. Their hearts have been grieved at the neglect of their brethren to send them any aid. While the Methodists have told them, You may as well join our society, for you never will see a preacher of your own denomination here. Many have complied with this advice—but some have remained steadfast. When they saw us, they shed tears of joy. In that part of the Territory that lies on the Wabash, there are settlements, both above and below Vincennes, that deserve the attention of missionary bodies, particularly those above, on Bussaron. An immense number of settlers have been crowding out on that frontier during the last season. We have now given a brief view of the principal settlements in the Indiana Territory. If one or two faithful Missionaries could be sent into it, to travel through it, and search it out—to collect congregations and organize churches—who can tell how much good might be done? They might become the fathers of the churches there. Thousands would rise up hereafter and call them blessed.

The ILLINOIS TERRITORY, when the last census was taken, contained 12,000 inhabitants. Its present population may be about 15,000. The hostilities of the neighbouring savages have prevented any very considerable increase. Until the last summer, titles of land could not be obtained in this Territory. But now Land Offices are opened —and some portions of the country are extremely fertile. It is probable, therefore, that settlers will now begin to flock in, especially if the war should soon terminate. The principal settlements in the Territory, at present, are situated on the Ohio, and the Wabash, and on the Mississippi, and the Kaskaskias. The eastern settlements are considerably extensive, spreading 30 miles up the Wabash, and 40 down the Ohio. They include the U. S. Saline, where a considerable number of people are employed in manufacturing salt, to the amount of 3,600 bushels a week. Of this county, Shawanee-town is the seat of justice. It contains about 100 houses, situated on the Ohio, 12 miles below the entrance of the Wabash, and subject to be overflowed at high water. But it is continually deluged like most other towns in the Territories, by a far worse flood of impiety and iniquity. Yet even here a faithful missionary might hope to be extensively useful. The people heard us with fixed and solemn attention, when we addressed them. The western settlements in this Territory are separated from the eastern by a wilderness of 100 miles. They lie in a country highly interesting, considered as missionary ground. The American Bottom is an extensive tract of alluvial soil on the bank of the Mississippi, 80 miles in length, and about 5 in breadth. This land is endowed with a surprising and an exhaustless fertility. It is capable of supporting, and is doubtless destined to receive an immense population. The high lands back are also extremely fertile. Kaskaskias is the key to all this country: and must therefore become a place of much importance, although at present it does not greatly flourish. It contains between 80 and 100 families, two thirds French Catholics. The people of this place are very anxious to obtain a Presbyterian clergyman. Gov. Edwards assured us, that a preacher of popular talents would receive a salary of $1000, per annum, for preaching a part of the time, and instructing a small school. By giving another portion of his services to the people of St. Genevieve he might obtain an addition of 2 or 300 dollars. Six miles from Kaskaskias there is an Associate Reformed congregation of 40 families. Besides this we did not hear of a single organized society of any denomination in the county, nor of an individual Baptist or Methodist preacher. The situation of the two upper counties is in this respect somewhat different. Baptist and Methodist preachers are considerably numerous; and a majority of the heads of families, as we were informed by Gov. Edwards and others, are professors of religion. A Methodist minister told us that these professors were almost all of them educated Presbyterians. And they would have been so still, said he, had they not been neglected by their eastern brethren. Now they are Baptists and Methodists. How many of them could be restored to the Presbyterian connexion by a prudent and pious missionary, it is impossible to say. In all this Territory there is not a single Presbyterian preacher. And that is not all: when we arrived there we learnt that very considerable districts had never before seen one. Already have the interests of orthodoxy and of vital godliness suffered an irretrievable loss. And they must suffer more and more, until missionaries are employed and sent to erect the standard of the truth, and establish the institutions of the Gospel.

The MISSOURI TERRITORY is fast rising into importance, and is well worthy the attention of missionary societies. In 1810 it contained

3

little more than 20,000 souls. At present we have reason to believe, from information obtained from Gov. Clark, that this Territory has a population little short of 30,000. It has never been explored, as we could learn, by any person having its religious state and interests in view. Our remarks, therefore, except with respect to those parts visited by us, cannot be very particular. In St. Louis and its neighborhood, the call is extremely urgent for a clergyman. It contains about 2,000 inhabitants;—one third perhaps are Americans, the remainder French Catholics. The American families are many of them genteel and well informed; but very few of them religious. Yet they appear to be thoroughly convinced, by their own experience, of the indispensable necessity of religion to the welfare of society. When we told them that a missionary had been appointed to that station by the Connecticut Missionary Society, they received the information with joy. And they are anxiously expecting his arrival. The most respectable people in town assured us, that a young man of talents, piety, and *liberality* of mind, would receive an abundant support; 12 or 1400 dollars a year might be relied on by such a man; if he would teach a school and preach but a part of his time. The remainder might be devoted to the neighbouring settlements. When we consider the present situation of St. Louis, and the high probability that it will become a flourishing commercial town; we cannot but earnestly desire, that the person already appointed, or some other suitable one, may speedily be sent to occupy this important post. Situated just below the confluence of the Illinois, the Mississippi and the Missouri; no place in the Western country, New Orleans excepted, has greater natural advantages. No place, therefore, has higher importance, considered as a missionary station.*

Next to St. Louis in point of importance, is St. Genevieve. It lies one mile from the Mississippi, including New Bourbon about two miles distant; it has a population of 1500. There are about 25 American families; the remainder French. A missionary visiting this place occasionally, would be well received, and would obtain a considerable part of his support. While a person acting in the double capacity of preacher and instructor of the Academy in that place, would receive a salary of $1000 per annum. Respecting the religious state of the other towns and villages in the Territory, we have no definite information. It should speedily be inquired into by a missionary on the ground. There are also many American settlements throughout the country, that require to be sought out, and to have congregations organized, where they are capable of it. Among which are the following: The settlements in the neighborhood of the lead mines are very considerable. At Mine a Burton (40 miles west from St. Genevieve) there is a village of 20 families. When the people of that place heard that we were in the Territory, so anxious were they to obtain a Presbyterian preacher, that they circulated a paper, and immediately procured subscriptions to the amount of $200 for a missionary who would visit that place occasionally. Mr. Austin, originally from New-England, sent us a pressing invitation to come and preach there. But

* See Appendix, F.

that was impracticable, and their hopes were for the present disappointed. These settlements are certainly interesting in a missionary point of view. The annual produce of the mines, two years since, was 1,525,000lbs. of lead. The number of persons employed in digging, smelting, &c. is at present very great, and will doubtless increase with rapidity. On the Saline, 5 miles from St. Genevieve, is an American settlement of about 50 families; some are Presbyterians. At the Bois Brule bottom on the Mississippi, 15 miles below St. Genevieve, are about 30 American families. There is also a settlement on the Platen, and a large one of 150 or 200 families on the St. Francis. Toward the North West from St. Louis, very considerable settlements are scattered up the Mississippi, the Missouri, and their tributary streams, for near 200 miles. When we were in the Territory, we could not learn that any Presbyterian minister had ever before preached there; yet most of its settlements are frequently visited by Baptist and Methodist preachers. There was even a man of the New England sect of *Christ*-ians* preaching and distributing books in this and the adjacent Territory.

In addition to the above detailed account of these Territories, we have a few general remarks to offer, applicable to them all. The character of the settlers is such as to render it peculiarly important that missionaries should early be sent among them. Indeed, they can hardly be said to have a *character*; assembled as they are from every State in the Union, and originally from almost every nation in Europe. The majority, although by no means regardless of religion, have not yet embraced any fixed principles or sentiments respecting it. They are ready to receive any impressions which a public speaker may attempt to make. Hence every species of heretics in the country flock to the new settlements. Hence also the Baptist and Methodist denominations are exerting themselves to gain a footing in the Territories. If we do not come forward and occupy this promising field of usefulness, they will. Indeed they have already taken the precedence. Some portions of this country are pretty thoroughly supplied with their preachers. Why, then, it may be asked, should we not leave it wholly to them? We answer, the field is large enough for us all. Many of their preachers are exceedingly illiterate. And this circumstance, if some of the most respectable inhabitants may be credited, has been a very great injury to the cause of Christ in many places. Besides, there are many Presbyterian brethren, scattered throughout almost every settlement. And to supply them with the stated means of grace, so far as we are able, is a sacred duty incumbent upon us. We have already mentioned a number of places, in which an earnest desire was manifested to have missionaries sent among them. This was not the desire of a few individual Presbyterians merely; but of many of the officers in the civil government of the Territories, and of some of the most respectable citizens of various denominations. The three Governors and a number of the judges, in the respective Territories, expressed to us their feelings upon this subject. Gov. Edwards of Illinois has been for some time endeav-

---

* The sect of Elias Smith.

ouring to obtain a Presbyterian preacher there ;—and Gov. Posey of Indiana proposed himself to write to some missionary Society to obtain one for his neighbourhood. To be supported by the countenance and patronage of such men would be a vast advantage to a preacher. Are not the fields then white already to the harvest? Would that all Christians at the East would lift up their eyes and behold. Could they but see what we have seen—thousands ready to perish, their eye-lids fast closed in spiritual slumber, and no one to awake them— Could they but see the sons and daughters of Jerusalem weeping for themselves and for their children ;—surely missionaries would no longer be wanting, nor funds for their support.

If missionaries could by any means be sent into these Territories, there are various other ways in which they could be extensively useful, besides their ordinary labours, in preaching and administering the ordinances of the Gospel. This country is almost wholly new ground. Many institutions that conduce to the benefit of Society, and to the advancement of religion, are not yet established. Much good might be done by exerting an influence in favour of schools, and of the education of children. An inhabitant of the Eastern States can have no adequate conception of the want of schools in this country. It is very common to find men of considerable property, whose children cannot read a word. Much good might also be done by a missionary, in promoting the establishment and success of Bible Societies, and of other moral and religious institutions. In our former communications, we have made you, in some measure, acquainted with the dreadful famine of the *written*, as well as *preached* word of God, which prevails in this country. We have also laid before you an account of our exertions and success in promoting the establishment of associations for the distribution of the Scriptures. Should these associations be organized, still they will need some fostering hand to support and render them efficient: otherwise many years will roll away before the sacred oracles will be found in every dwelling. The success with which we were favoured, altogether surpassing our most sanguine expectations, proves that the happiest consequences might be expected from vigorous and persevering exertions in promoting this grand object. Such missionaries should be well supplied with Bibles and Religious Tracts for gratuitous distribution. Undoubtedly they would be so by Societies in the Atlantic States. In this way their usefulness would be extended far beyond the sphere of their personal exertions. We are confident, that our present mission is rendered far more useful than it would otherwise be, by the Bibles and Tracts with which we are furnished. Our Bibles are of course beneficial. Our Tracts (chiefly of the collection published by the New England Tract Society,) have been received and read with eagerness. They have been handed from house to house ; and have been approved, so far as we can learn, by all denominations. Such publications are so scarce in this country, that attention is secured to them by that powerful principle—the love of novelty. Sectarian jealousies and even political prejudices against New England have promoted the circulation and perusal of our Tracts. *Can any good thing come out of Nazareth? Come and see.*

Perhaps, dear Sir, we have already stepped beyond our proper limits. Our appropriate business is, to collect information, and state facts; not to draw conclusions, nor attempt to direct our fathers in the ministry, and missionary bodies, with respect to their duty. But we must ask your indulgence a little farther. From the view we have now given of the three Territories, it is apparent, that at least one missionary to each of them is indispensably requisite. If one or two more could by any means be obtained, there would be some peculiar advantages in the following distribution of them. The settlements in Indiana lie principally on the Eastern and on the Western sides of the Territory. A wilderness of about 100 miles intervenes. The same is the case in Illinois. The Eastern settlements in Indiana are sufficiently extensive to require the whole time of a missionary. While the Western settlements of this Territory and the Eastern of Illinois, that is the country on both sides of the Wabash, might for the present be supplied by the same preacher. The other portions of Illinois on the bank of the Mississippi, seem to demand a distinct labourer. And the Missouri Territory should have one, if not two more. Considering the importance of St. Louis, it seems highly desirable, that one faithful man should be posted there, to labour in that place and its immediate vicinity; while another might be advantageously employed at St. Genevieve, the Mines, and other settlements in the Territory.

It seems desirable that missionaries in this country should pay particular attention to the towns and villages. They are much more destitute of religious privileges than the back settlements. The Baptist and Methodist preachers of this country find but little encouragement to visit them. The inhabitants of the towns having been long freed from the restraints of religion, have become much more vitiated in their morals, than those of the country. The character of Shawanee-town we have mentioned, not as in this respect singular; but as a specimen of almost all of them. Yet in these places there are many friends of good order and religion, who would hold up the hands of a respectable and pious minister. In these places we behold the germs of future cities. The village, that now contains nothing but log cabins, will soon become the dwelling place of thousands. And those thousands may all be favourably affected by the early establishment of religious institutions there.

And now, dear Sir, we commend into the hands of your Society their brethren in the west. We have done what we could for them. We have endeavoured to represent their wretched condition. We have conveyed to your ears their earnest cries for aid. And surely, if there be any bowels and mercies, their cries will not be heard in vain. It is not the voice of strangers and foreigners. They are members of the same civil community with us. Many of them are fellow citizens with the saints and of the household of God. Some once enjoyed with delight the Sabbaths, and sermons, and sacraments of New England. And their hearts still retain the relish. Their eyes are constantly looking towards the East. Their prayers ascend daily, that God would incline the hearts of their brethren to remember them, and send them one to break to them the bread of life. But the answer of their prayers is long deferred; and their heart often sickens within them. By sending us among them, you have shown that they are not indeed forgotten, and have inspired them with a cheering hope. Shall that hope be grievously disappointed?

Yours with affection and respect, &c.

VI. *View of Kentucky and Tennessee.*

On the Mississippi, above Natchez, Feb. 1, 1815.

Rev. and Dear Sir,—The last communication we made to you, relative to the Mission on which we are engaged, was dated January 20th. We then gave you a view of the Territories, Indiana, Illinois and Missouri, contemplated as fields for Missionary labour. We left the Territories the latter part of November. The month of December we spent principally in Lexington, Frankfort and Louisville, *Ken.* As the state of morals and religion, in this portion of our country, was noted with some degree of particularity, in the *Correct View,* referred to in our last letter, we shall add but a few things.

The greater part of this State may be considered as a proper missionary field. Some of the counties, containing from 10 to 12,000 inhabitants, have not a Congregational or Presbyterian minister within their limits. In these counties, as in almost all parts of our western country, there are many Presbyterian families, and more or less who formerly belonged to churches of that order. They deeply lament the loss of privileges they once enjoyed; and would receive a pious, evangelical Missionary, as one who brought to them glad tidings of great joy.*—A Missionary would no doubt be very useful, not only as a preacher of the gospel to the scattered lambs of the flock, but also in aiding the funds of the Bible Society of that State, and in supplying the destitute with the sacred Scriptures.—Religious Tracts might likewise be committed to his care for distribution. And it would be an object with him to inquire after pious young men, and encourage them to prepare for the ministry.†

The managers of the Kentucky Bible Society (as it is now called) have as yet had at their disposal but small resources. Their ability however, to forward the object for which they are associated, is increasing. They have contributed $200, to assist the New York Bible Society, in printing an edition of the Bible in the French language. At the present time, we have reason to believe, the Bible is possessed by but comparatively few of the families in the State. Of the 600 Bibles committed to our care by the Bible Society of Mass. 100 were left in this State for distribution. Fifteen hundred Religious Tracts were distributed, a part by us, and a part were committed to the care of others to give out.

* The Trustees of the Connecticut Missionary Society have lately received a communication from certain clergymen of respectability in Kentucky, earnestly requesting, that they would send on a Missionary, to be employed in that State. We believe the request will be granted, as soon as a proper character shall be found.

† There is a Female Charitable Society in Lexington, who support two young men in the Theological Seminary at Princeton.

From extracts of letters in our possession,* it will appear, that the want of Bibles and Religious Tracts is very great in this State. Throughout the western country, the call is much more pressing than the religious public, in the older states, have been accustomed to suppose. Could the true state of the destitute be presented, funds, we are persuaded, to a much larger amount would be contributed, to extend to them more effectual relief. The state of Kentucky, according to the last census, had a population of more than 400,000 souls. *Thirty thousand* Bibles are probably wanted to supply all the destitute families. There are about 80,000 people of colour, principally slaves, within the limits of the State. It is very rare that a Bible can be found in the possession of any of them, though many of them can read; and were they possessed of it, many more would soon learn. One of the managers of the Bible Society informed us, that he had given a few Bibles to these people; and that they had received them with tears of joy. They invoked the blessing of God, on those, who furnished the Bibles for distribution, and on the distributors. They said they valued them more than all things else of which they were possessed. Have not these blacks peculiar claims upon us ? If their cries for the Word of Life do not enter into our ears; still they will into the ears of that God, who hears the ravens when they cry; and he may visit us in judgment for neglecting them.

The advocates for infidel principles, in this part of our country, are much less bold, and much less active, in propagating their sentiments, than they were a few years ago. Publications, calculated to give currency to their tenets, we were led to believe, are generally neglected. The present seems to be a favourable time, to attempt religious charitable exertions among the people.

The formation of a Foreign Missionary Society, among the Baptists in an important part of the State, has had an evident tendency, not only to render less frequent the bickering and debate among those of that order; but has likewise been the means of removing many, to say the least, unkind prejudices, which before were felt toward other denominations. This spirit of Christian charity appears to be increasing.

At Lexington there is building a second Presbyterian church. The prospect is, that a respectable congregation will soon be collected, under the care of the Rev. Mr. M'Chord. At Frankfort, the seat of government for the State, a handsome church has been erected, and nearly completed. Those attached to the Presbyterian connexion, did not know whom they could obtain to settle with them. At Louisville, during our stay, a number of the citizens gave an invitation to the Rev. Gideon Blackburn to settle with them. They engaged to secure to him one thousand dollars a year, for his services a part of the time. When not occupied in that place, he would be at liberty to supply other vacant congregations in the vicinity. A committee was chosen, to make arrangements for building a Presbyterian church. A disposition was manifested by a number of gentlemen of the place, to aid the object by their liberal donations. We have since been informed, that Mr. Blackburn will not comply with their request. The

* See Appendix, G.

place we conclude is vacant. Both Frankfort and Louisville are very important stations. It is much to be desired, that men of piety and talents might soon be introduced into them. A very happy influence would doubtless be exerted by them on the vacant country around.

As we did not visit TENNESSEE, we have little to say concerning its present state. Both East and West Tennessee present extensive Missionary fields. By an estimate made about two years ago, it appears, that there were twenty five counties in the State, containing nearly 150,000 inhabitants, *without a Presbyterian minister in either of them.* The vices, common in our western country, prevail in this State,—intemperance—profanity—Sabbath breaking—gambling, &c.

More than two years since, there was a prospect, that a Bible Society would be formed in West Tennessee. Certain circumstances had, however, prevented its organization. When we heard last from Nashville, the object was still kept in view; and the contemplated Society will no doubt eventually succeed. The want of Bibles and other religious books in this State, is probably as great as in Kentucky. A respectable clergyman says—" Perhaps one fourth of our population has not a Bible." According to this estimate, which we think is too favourable, *more than ten thousand* Bibles are wanted, in order to give a copy to each destitute family.

Yours affectionately, &c.

VII. *View of the country from the falls of the Ohio to Natchez.*

Natchez, Mississippi Ter. Feb. 6, 1815.

Dear Sir,—There are no very considerable villages, between this place and the falls of the Ohio, a distance of more than twelve hundred miles. The banks of the Ohio and Mississippi are but partially settled. In descending these rivers, we have passed but one settlement, in which the word and ordinances of the gospel are statedly administered, by a Presbyterian clergyman. Baptist and Methodist preachers are to be met with occasionally. The *former*, in many instances, do not inculcate upon their hearers the importance of observing the Sabbath day as holy time. Neither do they enjoin upon parents the duty of religiously educating their children. The belief of the *latter* is well known. The religious sentiments of the inhabitants are very incorrect; and great stupidity, as it respects a concern for the salvation of the soul, appears generally to prevail. A reason, which answers in part for this inattention is obvious, *the people perish for lack of knowledge.*

Not only are the inhabitants destitute in a great measure of the word preached in its simplicity and purity, but it is a fact much to be lamented, that but comparatively few families are supplied with the Bible. Very many, who desire to possess such a treasure, know not how to obtain it. Others there are, who would receive the Bible as a gift, and return their thanks for it; who, unless supplied in this way, would probably spend their lives without reading a chapter, or scarcely knowing that there is such a book extant. It would be a

* See Appendix, H.

labour indeed, to ascertain precisely the number of Bibles wanted in a State or Territory, that every destitute family might be supplied. We can assert with safety, that but comparatively few are possessed of them.

At the mouth of the Cumberland river, there is a settlement of ten or twelve families. A person, who had resided there a number of years, observed, that very few if any of the families were supplied with the sacred Scriptures. A man, who had lived on the west bank of the Mississippi, some distance below the mouth of the Ohio, stated, that there were twelve or fourteen families settled near him; and it was his opinion, that there was not a Bible in any of their houses.— This settlement is composed principally of emigrants from the States. With respect to other religious books, but few can be found in the possession of the inhabitants. And a part of those are better calculated to disseminate error than the truth.

The country generally from the falls of the Ohio to Natchez is thinly settled. This circumstance renders it inconvenient for the people to support schools. And it is not unfrequently the case, that they know not the value of such institutions, even where they have ability to support them. The education of children therefore, is very much neglected; the few Spanish and French inhabitants, who reside on either bank of the Mississippi, are, if possible, more destitute of religious instruction than the Americans.

Perhaps the best means of giving religious instruction to the people in this district of country, is the distribution of Bibles and Religious Tracts. These might be committed to the care of certain gentlemen, who would make a judicious distribution of them; and who occasionally descend the Ohio and the Mississippi rivers to New Orleans. When we went on board the boat at the falls of the Ohio, we took with us a quantity of English Bibles, French Testaments, and Religious Tracts. A part of each was distributed to the destitute poor on the banks, as we passed down. We had many applications for the sacred Scriptures, with which we could not comply. Some of the people asserted, that they never had an opportunity to purchase the Bible at any price; though they had been long anxious to obtain it. Others were evidently too poor to furnish themselves without much inconvenience. The Bible was received by many, to whom it was presented, with an eagerness, which induced us to believe, that it would prove " a lamp to their feet, and a light to their path."

Before we left the falls, we received a box of 500 French Testaments. More than 250 copies, we directed to the care of Stephen Hempsted, St. Louis. Seventy five copies were sent to the care of the Rev. Mr. Scott of Vincennes. A number of copies were directed to a friend at Gallipolis, Ohio; and a few to Mr. Dufour, of Vevay, a French Swiss settlement in the Indiana Territory. We wrote to the gentlemen, to whom the Testaments were sent, stating from whence they came, and the manner in which they were to be distributed: requesting them to inform us by letter of the manner in which the Testaments were received.* At New Madrid, we ascertained

* See Appendix, I.

that there are between forty and fifty French families in that place. We were informed, that generally more or less in every family could read. As far as we could learn, none of them were supplied either with the Bible or Testament. We left a number of Testaments for distribution. There was a French school in the village, and the prospect was, that the Testaments would be introduced into it. We left a number of copies for another settlement, some miles below New Madrid on the bank of the river. We directed a supply to be sent to Ozark, a French village, containing between forty and fifty families, situated on the bank of the Arkansas river, some distance above its mouth. Without doubt much good will be effected by the circulation of the Testaments among the people. In addition to the moral and religious instruction, which we may reasonably expect they will derive from the sacred volume, numbers will be induced to learn to read, by means of this seasonable supply. The Religious Tracts were thankfully received. A more liberal distribution of them, we have reason to believe, would be attended with the happiest effects.

P. S. Feb. 11. Dear Sir, we arrived here on the 6th inst. in good health and spirits. The Lord is pleased to deal very graciously with us. We were for some time apprehensive, that the disturbed state of this country might embarrass us, in attending to the duties of our mission. But General Jackson has defeated and repulsed the British. They are still, however, hovering about the coast, and seem to meditate another attack—at what point is altogether uncertain. But we hope we shall be permitted to attend to the business of our Master's kingdom without molestation. On our arrival, we found the French Testaments consigned to this place had not been received. Mr. Mills therefore proceeded immediately to New Orleans, to learn if any had arrived there, that we might commence the distribution of them. May the Lord prepare the hearts of the French to receive them.

VIII. *View of the Mississippi Territory.*

New Orleans, March 13, 1815.

Reverend and Respected Friend,—We now proceed to give a brief account of the religious state of the Mississippi Territory. It affords a very interesting field for missionary labour. With a population of about 45,000, it has only four Presbyterian clergymen,—who divide their labours among ten congregations. They seem to be men of an excellent spirit. The Baptist denomination have in this Territory twenty nine churches; which are supplied by sixteen ordained and five licensed preachers. The number of persons in their communion is more than a thousand. The Methodist society has ten or twelve itinerant preachers in the Territory; and about a thousand members.

The city of Natchez is perhaps as important a station for a missionary, as any in the western or southern country. It contains about 2,500 inhabitants. It has an old Roman Catholic chapel, almost in ruins, a Methodist, and a new Presbyterian church. Some of the most respectable inhabitants are very desirous to obtain a Presbyterian preacher. In erecting the church the Trustees have exhausted their resources;—and there is reason to fear, that it will stand unoccupied; or that it will be diverted from its original design, and fall into the hands of men unfriendly to the truth. Present prospects in that place are hopeful. When Mr. Smith preached there the audiences were large and solemn. The Trustees of the church proposed to address themselves to your Society; and to request you to send them a missionary.* They said they would become responsible for his salary; and if he should be a man of popular talents and of piety, they presumed he would be immediately settled. A suitable person sent to this place would supply this church, would promote the interests of the Bible Society, which now languishes for want of such a patron, would become a bond of union to the scattered Presbyterian churches and ministers in the Territory, and would probably be the means of bringing in many more missionaries and ministers.

Other portions of this Territory might be pointed out, that afford promising fields for missionary labour. The south-western part of it, in particular, deserves immediate attention. The settlements in this quarter are very considerable. At Pinckneyville, on the Bayou Sara, a number of respectable gentlemen are very desirous to obtain a Presbyterian preacher. They think of erecting a church. And it is thought, that they would immediately afford a clergyman an adequate support. But they have no means of obtaining one; and will probably remain for years unsupplied; unless some one is sent to them from the Atlantic States.

The whole of this Territory is exceedingly destitute of the sacred Scriptures. Very few Bibles have ever been distributed in it. There is indeed at Natchez a pious gentleman who is a bookseller, and keeps Bibles on hand for sale. But many of the people live at a considerable distance from Natchez:—and very many of them are too poor, or too indifferent to religion to purchase. Indeed some are even ashamed to buy a Bible. When they ask for one at the bookstore, they often think it necessary to frame some frivolous apology for their conduct. The degraded Africans, although there are many individuals among them that can read, are almost without exception destitute of Bibles. The number of slaves in this Territory is about 20,000. And the Bible is almost the only book, that can be circulated among them without offence to their masters. We found on the bank of the Mississippi above Natchez, a slave, who seemed to love religion, and often recommended it to his comrades. Yet he had no Bible. We gave him one, and he received it with strong expressions of joy and gratitude. In many other parts of the Territory, there were persons who were very anxious to obtain the Scriptures. We could only refer them to the Mississippi Bible Society, for a supply.

This institution was established more than two years since, when Messrs. Schermerhorn and Mills visited Natchez. It came into existence under favourable auspices. His Excellency Governor Holmes

* This request has been received; and in consequence of it, the committee of the Society have determined to send Mr. Smith immediately into that portion of the country.

subscribed forty dollars towards its funds, and was elected President. Its subscriptions amounted to three hundred dollars. But ever since its first formation, it has languished for want of some active friend to attend to its concerns. Such a friend this Society would find, in a faithful missionary stationed at Natchez. The Managers have indeed distributed one hundred Bibles, presented to them by the New York Bible Society, and one hundred and twenty-five, forwarded by us, from the Mass. Bible Society. They have likewise prepared and circulated an interesting Report, calculated to arouse the attention of the public. But when we were there, they had made no very considerable collections of money; they had purchased no Bibles. *Five thousand* copies of the Scriptures, we believe, would not more than supply the destitute. Unless therefore some more efficient means are used to enlighten that benighted portion of our country, the day of glory will dawn upon the rest of the world, long before its darkness will be dispelled.

IX. *View of Louisiana.*

New Orleans, April 6, 1815.

Dear Sir,—The State of Louisiana, having lately become an integral part of the Union, deserves the attention of the public. It has imperious claim on the attention particularly of the religious public. The finger of Providence seems to be pointing this way. Recent events in this quarter at once arrest our attention and elevate our hopes. We refer to the late wonderful deliverance of this country from an invading foe; and to the subsequent distribution of a number of English Bibles and French Testaments. Perhaps there was, in the wisdom of divine Providence, a more intimate connexion between these events, than is obvious to the world. Even the most heedless and stupid of the inhabitants cannot but recognise the hand of God in the salvation of their country.—And perhaps they were thereby rendered more willing to give a favourable reception to the word of that God, who had so lately appeared for them in an hour of peril and distress.

In 1810 Louisiana contained 76,556 inhabitants; 34,660 of whom were slaves. Since that time its population is doubtless considerably increased: but to what amount, we are not able to say. The principal settlements, out of New Orleans, are the following. Those on the Mississippi, extending thirty miles below New Orleans, and above to the northernmost boundary of the State, are almost wholly occupied by Frenchmen, Acadians and Germans, who speak the French language. The settlements in the counties of Attakapas and Opelousas are very considerable; and have a mixture of French and American inhabitants. Those on the Red River are chiefly inhabited by Americans.—There are in this State two Methodist circuits; but there is no Baptist preacher, as we could ascertain; and out of New Orleans, no Presbyterian minister. A very large portion of the State has never, as we could learn, been visited by a Presbyterian preacher. Many of the American inhabitants were originally Presbyterians—and very many would rejoice to see a respectable missionary among them. It is therefore of immense importance, that some one should be sent to explore the country and learn its moral and religious state; and introduce, as far as possible, the institutions of the gospel. Such a man might not only be useful to the Americans; he might exert a very salutary influence on the French also. He would doubtless promote the farther distribution of the French Scriptures. Religious Tracts, in that language, might be very soon circulated among the people. And a prudent and diligent use of such means, we have reason to hope, would result in the happiest consequences.

In West Florida, the attention of some of the inhabitants was not long since called to the subject of religion. Many of them solicit for Bibles, whenever there is a prospect that they can be supplied, which is very rare. There are some American families, in this part of our country, *who never saw a Bible, nor heard of Jesus Christ.* There are some hopefully pious persons, who cannot obtain a Bible or Testament. These facts were given us by a religious teacher, who had been among the people of whom he spoke.

New Orleans would no doubt be the principal station of a Missionary sent into this State. It therefore deserves a description. When the census was taken it contained 24,552 inhabitants. At present it contains probably 30,000, as many as 12,000 of whom are blacks. And whether we consider its population, or its commerce, it ranks among the most important cities in the Union. More than half the white inhabitants are Frenchmen:—the remainder are Americans, from almost all the States;—and a few foreigners. Until lately the Romish religion prevailed to the exclusion of every other. But for some years past the city has been occasionally visited, by protestant preachers of different denominations. Mr. Chase of the Episcopal church was in the city three or four years, and established an Episcopal congregation. Mr. Hull, originally from Scotland, supplies this congregation at the present time. The only protestant place of worship in the city,* is an upper room in a building erected and owned by Mr. Paulding, a pious Baptist. This gentleman has devoted this room to the interests of evangelical religion. The state of public morals is extremely deplorable. Sabbath-breaking, profanity and intemperance prevail to a fearful extent. Yet there are in the city many respectable families, who are the friends of good order and morality. And there are some pious persons, who sigh daily for the abominations committed there. All these would hold up the hands of a faithful minister, as Aaron and Hur did the hands of Moses:—and it may be, that the hosts of Israel, though few and scattered, through the blessing of God, would prevail.

The Louisiana Bible Society was established at New Orleans, more than two years since, when Messrs. Schermerhorn and Mills visited this city. Already has this Society, although its internal resources have been small, done much to promote the interests of religion, in this State. It has aided in distributing 300 English Bibles,

* " *New Orleans, Aug.* 1.—On Thursday last, the 27th ult. the corner stone of a Protestant Church was laid in this city. We hope that piety and morals will flourish under the benign influence of the Great Author of all good ; that the people will acknowledge the great and important truth, that ' *It is righteousness alone that exalteth a nation.*' " (N. Eng. Palladium.)

the donation of the New York and Mass. Bible Societies,—and it has given out near 3,000 French New Testaments.* But still this Society needs the fostering care and the active services of some missionary man. It is a fact that ought not to be forgotten, that so lately as last March, *a Bible in any language could not be found, for sale or to be given away, in New Orleans.* And yet *eight thousand* Bibles would not supply the destitute in this State.

Our appeal is to the christian public. What shall be done? Shall we leave one of our fairest cities to be completely overwhelmed with vice and folly? The dreaded inundation of the Mississippi would not be half so ruinous. *Now* by divine assistance, an effectual barrier may be opposed to the flood of iniquity. And is the liberality of the christian community exhausted? Have you no Bibles to give: no missionaries to send? Are there no men of apostolic spirit, who desire not " another man's line of things made ready to their hands?" Then is the case of this city wretched and hopeless indeed.—But surely the cry of some of its citizens must be heard. It is earnest and importunate. It is continually sounding in our ears—Send us some one to break to us the bread of life.

Your affectionate friends and fellow servants in the gospel.

X. *Communication, relative to the distribution of English Bibles: from Mr. Mills.*

New Orleans, April 18, 1815.

Dear Sir,—You will recollect that Mr. Smith and myself arrived at Natchez on the sixth of February. He remained some weeks in that place, and the adjacent country, labouring to strengthen the hands of the righteous few.

I came on to this place on the tenth of February. I brought with me one hundred and fifty English Bibles. One of the managers of the Louisiana Bible Society had on hand about forty more. Near two hundred Bibles were ready for distribution when I arrived in the city.

Some circumstances, attending the distribution of these Bibles, may be interesting to the Trustees of your Society.—The principal facts, which I shall present, are taken from my journal.

Feb. 10. This morning I called upon Esq. Hennen; and concluded, at his request, to take lodgings with him for the present. I called in company with Mr. H. at the public prison; there are three hundred English soldiers in the prison. A number of Bibles had some time since been distributed among them, by one of the managers of the Society. We found many of them reading, with great attention and seriousness, the copies which had been furnished them. We gave them some additional supply. They received the Bibles with evident expressions of joy and gratitude. We distributed among them likewise a number of Religious Tracts and Sermons. They returned many thanks for them. More or less of the soldiers are, it is

* For the particulars, we refer you to the succeeding communications, and to the Report of the Louisiana Bible Society. See Appendix, K.

said, apparently pious men. They informed us, that many of them were furnished with Bibles or Testaments, but left them on board the fleet. In the course of the same day, we called upon Dr. Dow. He informed us, that he had furnished some of the prisoners with a num- of Watts's Psalms, and some other religious books.

The succeeding day, I called at the United States Hospital, in company with Esq. Nicholson. There are three hundred men sick and wounded, in the Hospital;—one hundred and eighty are English prisoners. Upon examining the several wards, we found that some of the prisoners had brought their Bibles from the fleet; but this was rarely the case. A number of the sick and wounded, both English and Americans, expressed an earnest desire to be possessed of the sacred Scriptures.—Called at the Navy Hospital, containing about forty sick. There was not a Bible among them, as we could learn ; but more or less will thankfully receive them. We called at three different places, where a part of the sick soldiers, belonging to the Kentucky detachment are quartered. The whole number of sick at these houses is one hundred and twenty. Many of them received the information with great satisfaction, when informed that some of them could be furnished with Bibles. This was manifest, from their coun- tenances, and from the numerous applications, which were made for this blessed book. In one of the houses, we found a number of the sick lying on the floor. One was reading from a New Testament to those around him.—They had not a Bible in the house.

On the 12th, In the morning, I called with a friend at the Charity Hospital. There are forty sick soldiers at this Hospital, belonging to the Tennessee troops. They had not a copy of the sacred Scrip- tures. A number were very pressing in their solicitations, that we would supply them. We observed to them, that they would prob- ably soon leave the Hospital for Tennessee ; and as they expect- ed to travel on foot eight hundred or a thousand miles, they could not carry their Bibles with them, should they be supplied. Some of them answered at once, that they would leave some other articles, rather than their Bibles. Upon our return, we sent a number of Bibles to the hospital. We called at three different places, which we visited yesterday, occupied by the sick belonging to the Kentucky de- tachment; and distributed among them seventeen Bibles. They were thankfully received. The minds of many of the sick appear to be solemnly affected. We hope there are some godly persons among them. We explained to them the object of the Bible Society; and charged those who received copies of the Bible, to make a good use of them.

13th. We sent a number of Bibles to a fourth house occupied by about forty sick Kentucky soldiers; and received many thanks for them. Visited a house occupied by the sick troops from Tennessee; there were one hundred sick at this house, but not a Bible among them all. We left one in each room. Visited the United States Hospital, and distributed thirty Bibles among the destitute. Many applications were made for the sacred Scriptures, with which we could not comply. It is sickly at the present time. Since the 8th of January, a great mortality has prevailed. Twenty and even thirty of our soldiers have died in a day.

15th. I have ascertained that there are a considerable number of the troops belonging to the militia of this State, who are sick in hospitals, on the opposite side of the river. It is the impression of many, who go to the hospitals, that they shall die in them. This impression perhaps hastens their dissolution in some instances.

16th. We visited a hospital occupied by the Tennessee troops. One hundred are sick at this place. They had no Bibles in the house. Found a few leaves of the Old Testament in the possession of one of the soldiers. Distributed among them fourteen Bibles. They were very thankfully received.

17th. To day there was a meeting of the managers of the Bible Society. They voted their thanks to the societies that had generously aided them by donations in Bibles. Visited one of the hospitals, prayed with and addressed the sick in two of the wards. A sick man from Tennessee appeared to be much exercised in his mind. He seemed conscious of his ruined state by nature, and of the necessity of his exercising repentance toward God, and faith in the Lord Jesus Christ, in order to obtain the salvation of his soul. The sick appeared much gratified by the attention paid them.

18th. I visited to day, in company with Mr. N. one of the hospitals, at which we had previously called, and in which we had left a few copies of the Bible. Some of the men had died since our first visit to them; and others had so far recovered as to be able to leave the house; and their places had been supplied by the sick, brought in from the camp. We found a number of the rooms containing eight or ten sick, without a copy of the sacred Scriptures. Supplied one copy to each room, and received many thanks.

22nd. I crossed the River to day, and visited the sick soldiers in the barracks. In two rooms, there were near one hundred sick. It is truly affecting to visit these abodes of disease and death. The sick have not generally beds or mattresses. With medical aid, they are tolerably well furnished; still no doubt many of them suffer much, for the want of proper attendance. In some instances, when I have been addressing the sick in one room; I could hear those in the room adjacent, crying out with great earnestness—Lord, have mercy on us:—Jesus Christ, have mercy on us. I informed those I visited that there were some Bibles on hand to be given to the sick and the destitute. There were many applications for them. During my stay at the barracks I was at six or eight of the rooms. There was not a Bible to be found in any of them. I have found unusual freedom, in speaking to the sick and the dying in the hospitals. They almost uniformly give very strict attention to what is said; and their tears witness for them that they do not remain unaffected. God only knows, how lasting their serious impressions may be. But from what I have seen and heard in the hospitals, I am inclined to believe, that some of the sufferers have been born again, even on the threshold of the grave. Many of the troops, after their arrival in the vicinity of this place, were subjected to great fatigue while defending the lines. Many of them were standing or lying, for some successive days and nights, in the low marshy ground where the water was near a foot deep. The weather some of the time was so cold, as to freeze ice a quarter of an inch in thickness.—Some of the soldiers at this time were but poorly clothed—three or four physicians from Kentucky and Tennessee have died but a short time since.

23d. This morning more than four hundred English prisoners left this place. They went on board the steam boat and two sloops which were to carry them to the fleet, or the proper vessel prepared to receive them lying off the mouth of the river.

After their departure, I called at the prison, and obtained leave of the keeper, to examine the rooms, which had been vacated by the prisoners, in order to ascertain whether any of the Bibles we had distributed were remaining in them. But not a Bible had been left, nor the remnant of a Religious Tract. The Prisoners had retained them all. The servant informed me that he saw them packing them up in their knapsacks, a little time previous to their departure.

From the manner in which the prisoners received the Bibles, and from the care with which they preserved them, we have reason to believe, they will be very serviceable to many of them.

25th. This morning I crossed the river to visit the sick soldiers in the barracks, now converted into hospitals. There are three hundred and sixty in the barracks. Some of them are dangerously ill. Five or six died the last night. I went into a number of the rooms, containing each from thirty to forty sick. In one room at which I called, there was a corpse lying on the floor, partially wrapped in a blanket. One person appeared to be in the agonies of death, apparently insensible to every thing around him. Others were groaning and calling for assistance. A number came in from the adjacent rooms. I addressed those present and prayed with them, they were attentive and solemn. In five of the rooms I left ten Bibles. Many of them appeared in some measure rightly to estimate the precious book.—The gratitude they manifested, upon the reception of the Bibles, was an ample reward for the exposure and labour attendant on furnishing them. Previous to this distribution, there was not a single copy of the Bible to be found, as I could learn, among near four hundred men in the barracks. After leaving the sick now referred to, I passed a number of additional rooms, containing sick soldiers. Near one of the rooms I observed three dead bodies, wrapped in blankets. The deceased died in the same room during the last night. But few of the dead I believe are buried in coffins. Before I left the barracks, I became acquainted with Gen. Morgan, who has the command of the militia of this State.—I saw likewise Dr. G. and Dr. R. who are the two principal physicians in this department. They sent two men with me to obtain an additional number of Bibles, for those rooms which as yet remained unsupplied. I sent back by them twenty-four; making in the whole thirty-four distributed in the barracks.

I lately visited the camp, occupied by the Kentucky detachment. Gen. Thomas informed me, that out of about 2,000 men belonging to this detachment, there were at the present time 800 on the sick list. The Kentucky troops are not supplied with even a single chaplain,

5

while there are four attached to the troops from the State of Tennessee. I have ascertained that there are three or four houses near the camp (which is three miles below the city,) containing sick soldiers, which have as yet received no supply of Bibles. The officers are I believe uniformly attentive to the sick belonging to their several detachments.

27th. This morning I crossed the river to visit the sick in the barracks. Dr. G. introduced me to one of the sick under his care. He wished me to converse with him. The sick man professed to hope, that he was made a subject of the renewing grace of God about three years since. He readily acknowledged his lost and ruined state by nature, and professed his confidence in Jesus Christ, as the great atoning sacrifice. He remarked that he had no fears of death. He said he felt happy to be in the hands of a good and merciful God, and was willing to be at his disposal. He professed the fullest confidence in the rectitude of the divine government, and would endeavour to trust in the Lord. He added that he had an aged and infirm mother, who looked to him for support and consolation; and if it should please heaven, he could wish to recover, in hopes of relieving her sorrows, as she descended into the vale of years. After conversing with the sick man, I addressed those present. A number came in from the adjoining rooms. We sang and closed with prayer. The season was a very solemn one,—many were in tears.

March 1st. To day I crossed the river to visit the sick. During my stay, preached to more than 200 of the soldiers, who were able to assemble. The meeting was a solemn and interesting one. Dr. G. and Dr. R. expressed their thanks for the attention paid to those under their care. They wished to have their thanks presented to the managers of the Bible Societies, who had furnished them with the sacred Scriptures.

One of the chaplains belonging to the Tennessee detachment, informed me lately, that most of the intemperate men from that State had died since they came here; his expression was, The hard drinkers are nearly all gone.

5th. To day I visited one of the hospitals. The soldiers had so far recovered from their sickness, as to be able to join their fellows in the camp.

The hospital is now principally occupied, by the needy and the sick from the city. The soldiers who have left the hospital have taken their Bibles with them, and there are a number of needy people in it, without any supply.

7th. I called to day at one of the houses occupied by the Kentucky sick soldiers. Some of them have been a long time sick, but appear to be recovering. Numbers are still dangerously ill; they lie around the floor in all directions—some groaning and some praying;—they however gave very strict and solemn attention, while I addressed them and prayed with them. It was the first serious address and prayer, that numbers of them had heard since they left home, and perhaps for years.—When I was about leaving the room, one of the men, as he lay on the floor, reached out his hand and grasping mine, exclaimed, "God bless you—God bless you." I entered into conversation with him; and ascertained, that for some time past he had entertained a hope that he had been born again. After conversing with him freely, I left him with a request to examine himself as in the presence of the heart-searching God, who could not be deceived and would not be mocked. What will be the result of exertions to relieve the wretched in these abodes of misery—these cages of despair, God only knows. He hath the hearts of all men in his hands, and here our hopes rest.

10th. To day, in company with Mr. Smith, I called at one of the hospitals, and made some inquiries respecting the Bibles, which had been left there some time since. There were two rooms containing the sick; only one Bible was remaining in each.

11th. This morning I rode down to the Kentucky camp. The Generals, Adair and Thomas, accompanied me. I had made a previous appointment to preach at the camp at ten o'clock, A. M. The notice had been given to the soldiers, and arrangements made. The place for preaching was in the open field. A platform was prepared for the speaker to stand on, raised six or eight feet from the ground. A large congregation was collected in a short time. As many as eight hundred or a thousand soldiers were present. They behaved with great propriety during the service—were solemn and attentive.

From the preceding account you will perceive, that we have reason to believe, the circulation of the Bibles among the suffering soldiers, was blessed to the spiritual benefit of many. We sincerely regret that there was not a greater quantity of Bibles at the disposal of the managers of the Bible Society. When the militia of this State were discharged, many of them called for Bibles to carry home with them. They came eight or ten in a company. These poor men, who had been jeopardizing their lives, on the high places of the field, in the defence of their country—whose health, in many instances, had been destroyed by the fatigues they endured—and some of whom were doubtless destined to fall by the way on their return to their homes, —requested that they might be furnished with Bibles. We informed them, that not a copy could be obtained. The deep regret, which they manifested on receiving this information, convinced us that they were sincere, well-meaning petitioners, and excited in our breasts emotions not to be described. But with an aching heart we sent them empty away, as we had done many of their fellows, who had previously applied.

We earnestly hope, that some more efficient means will be soon entered upon, which will meet the necessities of the destitute poor in this part of our country.   Yours affectionately, &c.

XI. *Communication, relative to the distribution of French Testaments, from Mr. Mills.*

Philadelphia, June 6, 1815.

Dear Sir,—The facts stated in this paper were contained in the report we made to the Philadelphia Bible Society. They give a partial view of the manner in which the French Testaments were received by the Roman Catholics in New Orleans, and its vicinity.

As has already been stated, I reached that place on the tenth of February. I soon ascertained that the 3000 copies of the Testament, directed to the care of the managers of the Louisiana Bible Society, had been received. But none of them had at that time been offered to the people. A few copies were given out on the day I arrived in the place. The succeeding day an additional number was distributed.

The day following, February twelfth, the number of the destitute, who made application for a supply, very much increased. From nine o'clock A. M. to one P. M. the door of the distributor was thronged with from fifty to one hundred persons. Those who applied were of all ages and of all colours. They were literally clamorous, in their solicitations for the sacred book. For some successive days the applicants became still more numerous. In a week after the distribution of the Testaments commenced, one thousand copies were given out. Some of those who requested a supply came prepared to purchase them. They remarked to the distributor that they must have a supply by some means. The Principal of the College, and a number of the instructors of the public schools in the city, presented written statements, containing a list of the scholars, under their care, who would make a profitable use of the Testaments, could the charity be extended to them. These statements were respectfully addressed to the distributor, with a request that as many of the scholars might be supplied, as was consistent with the views of the managers of the Society. Their solicitations were in most cases complied with.

Père Antonio, a leading character in the Roman Catholic church, in the city, very readily aided in the circulation of the Testaments among his people. Some more than two years ago, the Rev. Father engaged to assist in the distribution of French Bibles and Testaments. Soon after I arrived in the city I called upon him, in company with Mr. Hennen. We informed him that the Testaments had been received from the managers of the Philadelphia Bible Society; and presented him with a number of copies. He expressed great satisfaction, and repeatedly invoked the blessing of God on the donors. He observed that God would certainly bless the generous, pious men, who had exerted themselves to give to the destitute his holy word. He expressed his desire to obtain an additional number of copies, and engaged that he would make the most judicious distribution of them in his power. He remarked that he would give them to those persons, who would be sure to read them through.

After our visit to Antonio, his attendant called for two or three copies of the Testament. The man who attends at the cathedral was anxious to receive one. His choir of singers likewise requested a supply.

Soon after the distribution of the Testaments commenced, Mr. Hennen called upon Mr. Du Bourg, the administrator of the Bishopric, and informed him that the Testaments, printed by the managers of the Philadelphia Bible Society, had been received; and that some copies had been given to the people. The Bishop observed, that he had been made acquainted with the circumstance by some of his people, who had called upon him to ascertain, whether he would advise them to receive the Testaments. He added, that as they were not of the version authorized by the Catholic church, he could not aid in the distribution of them. When the distribution of the Testaments in the Convent was suggested, the Bishop remarked, that the parents of the children who received instruction at that place, were at liberty to furnish them if they thought best. I had myself an interview with the Bishop ; during our conversation, he expressed to me his regret that the Roman Catholic version of the Testament, printed in Boston in 1810, had not been followed, rather than the version printed by the British and Foreign Bible Society. He observed however, that he should prefer to have the present version of the Testament in the possession of the people, rather than have them remain entirely ignorant of the sacred Scriptures. I here state one or two incidents which occurred, as related by the Bishop, connected with the circulation of the Testaments.—A poor woman of his flock called on him, and handing him one of the Testaments—apparently with great anxiety, addressed him in the following manner : Good Father, what book is this ? The Bishop looking at it replied, Why, my child, it is the history of the Evangelists—it is the Gospel. I know that, replied the woman ; but is it a book you would recommend to your people ? Said the Bishop, It is a Protestant version ; it is as Calvin would have translated it. Good Father, replied the woman, keep the book, keep the book ! My child, answered the Bishop, you may retain the book, if you please. Read it with care ; and should you find any thing contrary to the Catholic faith, you will bear in mind that it is a Protestant version.

Miss J. one of the Nuns, called upon the Bishop somewhat agitated. She had been reading the Testament. Her mind was perplexed by the expression, in the summary of the first chapter of the First Epistle of St. John : " Et la confession de nos péchés à Dieu ;" *and the confession of our sins to God.* She had been taught that the confession of our sins was to be made to the priest ; or rather to God, as the Roman Catholics say, through or by the priest. She inquired what could be intended by the expression, *confession of our sins to God.* He informed her that the translation was a Protestant one, and that the expression she referred to was prefixed to the chapter by the translator. The Bishop remarked to me that he thought it not proper, that any explanations of the contents of the chapters should be prefixed to either Bibles or Testaments, designed for circulation among the Roman Catholics.

As early as the first of March, fifteen or sixteen hundred copies of the Testaments had been given out. Many of those who applied for them were very earnest in their requests. Some of them said, that they came in from the country, and could not be denied ; and some of them, that they had made repeated applications, without success. Some wished the Testaments for themselves ; some for a son or a daughter, and some were anxious to obtain a copy for each of their children. It was frequently the case, that numbers would remain a considerable time at the door of the distributor, after notice was given that no more Testaments would be given out until the succeeding day. Many applications were made by people of colour. We found that a much greater proportion of them, both old and young, could read intelligibly, than has generally been supposed.

A little previous to the attack of the English on New Orleans, three or four hundred free people of colour were organized into companies, for the defence of that place. A number of these men called for copies of the Testament. One of them wished to know, whether the officers of the companies, with whom he was connected, might be furnished each with a copy. He was answered in the affirmative, and informed that many of the privates could also be supplied. He expressed much surprise, that so many Testaments should be given away. He inquired from whence they came—whether they were the gift of the Legislature of the State, or of the General Government. He was informed that they were sent on by the managers of the Bible Society of Philadelphia. The object of the Society was explained to him. The gratuitous distribution of the Scriptures is a thing so novel in this part of our country, that it excites much surprise. There is probably a much greater proportion of the French people able to read, than has generally been supposed. The 5000 Testaments will furnish but a very partial supply.

Mr. K. one of the managers of the Bible Society, informed me, that an elderly woman, a Roman Catholic, called on him for a Testament. She remarked to him that she was very anxious to read it, and had applied several times to the Distributor for a copy, but without success. Mr. K. obtained one for her; she received it with tears of joy. She informed him, that when a girl her father had a book, which he valued much, and which he used to keep in a private manner. She thought it was the Bible—and for a long time had been desirous of obtaining it. She remarked, that now she had such a book as her father used to have.

Soon after my arrival at New Orleans, I had some conversation with a respectable planter, a Roman Catholic, respecting the circulation of the Testaments. He remarked to me, that he did not think a good Catholic had any occasion to read the Bible. Before I left that place, I ascertained that he had perused some portions of the Testament. And he informed a friend of his, that what he had read excited in his mind many reflections. A woman and her daughter came in from the Bayou St. John, two miles from the city. She informed the Distributor, that she had heard that there were Bibles and Testaments to be given to the destitute, and that she was hardly disposed to credit the report. She concluded, however, she would *"Come and see."*

In the Spring of 1811, eight or ten thousand of the inhabitants of St. Domingo came to this part of our country. Most of them remained in New Orleans. Many of them are about to return to St. Domingo, and will take with them the Testaments, where the sacred Scriptures have rarely if ever been introduced. Some copies have been sent to the Havanna on the island of Cuba.

On the first of April, in company with a friend, I set out upon a visit to the Attakapas country. We proceeded up the east bank of the Mississippi about eighty miles; then crossed the river and went in a westerly and south westerly direction, between fifty and sixty miles into the country. We often called at the houses by the way, distributed a number of Testaments in different parts of the country, and informed the people that a quantity had been sent on for gratuitous distribution by the Philadelphia Bible Society, and where they might apply to obtain them.

Have we not reason to hope, that in this region and shadow of death, the true light is beginning to shine? May it shine more and more until the perfect day.

For further particulars relative to the distribution of the Testaments, we refer you to the Report of the Louisiana Bible Society.*

XII. *Communication, respecting Spanish Testaments; addressed to one of the Managers of the Philadelphia Bible Society.*

Philadelphia, June 1, 1815.

Dear Sir,—In compliance with the request of the managers of your Society, communicated in your note of yesterday, we with pleasure present to them the information of which we are possessed, with respect to the destitute condition of the Spanish Roman Catholics in the State of Louisiana. During our stay in New Orleans, and while the French Testaments were circulating among the people; inquiries were frequently made for the Spanish Testament or Bible. It was the opinion of a number of gentlemen of information, that some hundreds of copies of the Testament might be readily distributed among the Spaniards, with a prospect that they would be gratefully received, and extensively useful. There are some extensive Spanish settlements in different parts of the State; but we have not been able to make out any satisfactory estimate of the number of Spanish inhabitants. There are many families on the Bayou La Fourche. Natchitoches on the Red river is partly settled by them, and there are a number of families in the vicinity of that place. We were informed that some hundreds of copies might probably be sent into New Spain, by the way of Natchitoches. Within the limits of Louisiana, five hundred copies of the Spanish Testament might probably be very soon distributed, and in a very satisfactory manner. Antonio de Sedilla (referred to in the preceding communication) expressed his readiness to aid in the distribution of the Spanish Testaments, within the limits of the State, should any number of copies be committed to his care for the purpose. He engaged likewise, should he be furnished with any considerable quantity, that he would send some to Havanna and some to Campeachy.

The Rev. Father has it in his power no doubt, to aid the circulation of the Scriptures in these places, and in other portions of Spanish America. The inhabitants of Cuba and of Campeachy have generally been esteemed very bigoted. If therefore the Testaments were permitted to circulate freely in these places, it is most likely that there would be no portion of the West Indies, or of Spanish country in North or South America, where the distribution of them would be forbidden. It is well known that many Provinces, formerly subject to the Spanish government, are at the present time in possession of the Revolutionists. No order of the Romish church could prevent the

* See Appendix, K.

circulation of the sacred Scriptures in these provinces. The present is certainly a very favourable opportunity for sending them to the places already named. Father Antonio informed us, that very many of the Spaniards could read. He said that they were required by the priests to read certain books made use of in their church; but that they were not supplied with the sacred Scriptures, of either the Old or New Testament.

As this paper presents to you the facilities for circulating the Spanish Testament not only within the limits of Louisiana, but also among the inhabitants of Cuba, New Spain and Campeachy; and of the adjacent countries; we would recommend that 1000 copies at least should be procured as speedily as possible, and directed to the care of the managers of the Louisiana Bible Society, either for gratuitous distribution, or in part for sale, as you shall think proper.

We shall close this communicatin with one or two extracts from our journals, relating to this subject. *New Orleans*, Tuesday 21 Feb. 1815. A gentleman called for a French Testament this morning, and remarked to Mr. Hennen that a few years since he was at Vera Cruz. While lying by at that port with his vessel, a Spaniard came on board, and observing an English Testament wished to know the price of it. The gentleman informed him that it was not for sale. The Spaniard was very anxious to have the owner set a price upon it. He said he could read English and had been anxious a long time to obtain a Bible or Testament. The gentleman at length let him have it at a moderate price. The Spaniard remarked that if he had charged him twenty dollars, or more than that sum, he would have given it.

The vessel in which Mr. Smith sailed from New Orleans put into Havanna in distress. Extracts from his journal while lying there. *Harbour of Havanna*, April 25, 1815. I hoped I should have an opportunity of making particular inquiries respecting the religious state of this city and island. But the excessive jealousy of these Dons has prevented. As soon as we entered the harbour a soldier was placed on board and the passengers were forbidden to go on shore. I have however walked through the principal streets of the city, and visited most of the churches. But I did not think it prudent to make many inquiries. I have only conversed with an American gentleman who has resided here many years, and a respectable Spanish merchant. They agree in opinion that the city and suburbs contain 130,000 inhabitants. They are almost all Spaniards, and of course Roman Catholics. If one might judge from the appearance of their churches on the Sabbath, there is no great attention even to the Romish religion among them. Their churches are very splendid, but the worshippers are few. The number of churches is five or six. There are four or five convents of Nuns, and several orders of Monks. How the Spanish Bible would be received, it is impossible to say; but that there is the greatest need of it is certain. The Spanish merchant I mentioned, told me that there were very few or no Bibles among the people; but he said, there were a great many other books. It is probable therefore that many of the Spanish can read. And it was his opinion that many of them would be glad to obtain the Scriptures.

We are, dear Sir, with sentiments of esteem, yours, &c.

XIII. *Communication, respecting the distribution of Religious Tracts.*

Andover, (Mass.) June 25, 1815.

Dear Sir,

In some of our previous communications, we have mentioned the distribution of Religious Tracts, conveyed into the western country by us. This was a very interesting part of our business, and deserves to be more particularly noticed.

When we started on the mission, we had at our disposal fifteen thousand Religious Tracts, of the selection published by the New England Tract Society. This Society had at that time, (although it was established but a few months before,) printed fifty different Tracts, on as many interesting, moral and religious subjects. All this variety we had with us. We had also a large quantity of sermons and pamphlets : among which were the following :—

Dr. Livingston's Missionary Sermon.
Dr. Dwight's   do.
Dr. Woods's   do.   { at the ordination of the Foreign Missionaries.
Dr. Woods's   do.   before the Mass. Miss. Society.
Dr. Worcester's   do.
Dr. Bogue's   do.   { occasioned by the death of Rev. Messrs. Cran, Brain, and Des Granges, in India.
Dr. Alexander's   do.
Mr. Horne's   do.
Mr. Emerson's   do.
Dr. Griffin's Charity Sermon.
Mr. Church's Sermon.
Mr. Beecher's Sermon preached at Hartford.
Mr. Beecher's Sermon preached at New Haven.
Mr. Payson's Discourse before the Bible Society of Maine.
Dr. Muir's Address to the Bible Society of Alexandria.
Dr. Backus's Address   { on the importance of reviving gospel discipline in the churches.
Mr. Emerson's Catechism.
Dr. Watts's   do.
Address on the evils of Intemperance, by the Fairfield Assoc.
Constitutions of moral and religious charitable Societies.
Reports of the Board of Commissioners for Foreign Missions.
Reports of the Bible Society of Philadelphia.
Horne's Letters on Missions.
Memoirs of Mrs. Harriet Newell, [50 copies.]

We were supplied with a considerable number of copies of each of the above pamphlets, and of many others. And we generally left a complete set of the Tracts, and many of the Sermons, with the clergymen we called upon ; and when an opportunity presented, we sent them to others upon whom we could not call. Neither the Tracts nor the Sermons were in the possession of any of the clergymen west of the mountains, with whom we became acquainted, until they were supplied by us. They expressed themselves highly gratified, upon receiving so many recent publications, so well calculated to make them acquainted with the signs of the times. It is hardly possible to conceive how destitute of this kind of information, respectable, pious people, and even clergymen are. There is but one religious periodical publication, in all the western country. A religious newspaper is published at Chillicothe, (Ohio) by the Rev. Mr. Andrews. If no other object was accomplished by our mission, besides the dispersion of the pamphlets, with which we were furnished; we should deem our time, and labour, and expense, amply compensated. This mode of doing good operates, in the first instance, upon ministers, and men of information. Some of them appear like men awaking at the dawn of day. Lately all was dark around them, and their eyes were shut. But now they are eagerly looking toward the *East*; and catching the first dawning rays of the Sun of righteousness, soon to arise and bless the nations.

On our way from Lexington to Louisville, in Kentucky, we called on a clergyman of our acquaintance. We had previously left with him a number of interesting papers, respecting Missionary, Bible, and Tract Societies. His views of such institutions appeared to be much enlarged. He was particularly pleased with the Tracts, as a means of doing good. He had been preaching to his congregations, respecting these institutions; and had frequently introduced into his discourses large extracts from the pamphlets, we had put into his hands. This information he said was highly interesting to his people. Often were they very much affected by it—even to tears. On one occasion, after he had been reading a Tract, an honest Dutchman came forward, and said, he wished to borrow that book; and he would have it translated into his own language, for the benefit of those who could not read English. The request was readily granted; and the Tract, entitled, "The Dairyman's Daughter," was put into the Dutchman's hand for translation.

For further interesting particulars, respecting the distribution of the Tracts, we must refer you to letters we have received from gentlemen in the western country.*

The Tracts were disposed of as follows:

Sent to Dr. Coffin, East Tennessee,	1,000
Left with gentlemen in Ohio, for distribution	2,200
in the Indiana Territory	900
in the Illinois Territory	600
in the Missouri Territory	600
in Kentucky	2,500
in West Tennessee	700
in the Mississippi Territory & Louisiana	1,500
Distributed by us	5,000
	15,000

A number of gentlemen at Lexington, Ken. expressed a wish, that there might be an edition of the Memoirs of Mrs. Newell printed in

* See Appendix, G.

that place. If permission could be obtained of the proprietor at Boston, they engaged to go forward with the work, and secure the profits of the edition, to aid some religious charitable object. Permission has been obtained; and by this means we hope this interesting work will soon be extensively circulated, in the western and southern country.

XIV. *Communication, respecting French Tracts.*

Andover, June 29, 1815.

Rev. Sir,—During our stay in New Orleans, our minds were much impressed with the importance of circulating Religious Tracts in the French language. Men of information, and those who have long been familiar with the French inhabitants of the State of Louisiana, requested us with great earnestness, to aid this object as far as we had ability. There are very few religious books or pamphlets to be found in their possession. A number of the Tracts, published by the New England Tract Society, were they translated into the French language, and sent into that country, would no doubt be eagerly sought after, and of infinite use among the people.

There are some considerations, which seem to urge this subject upon the attention of the religious public. The French people, Germans, Acadians and Spaniards, who compose a considerable part of the population of that State, have many of them of late years been fast inclining to intemperate habits. It was stated to one of us by a Roman Catholic priest, that previously to 1803, when the Americans took possession of that country, the people were in the habit of making use only of light wines; or that very little spirituous liquor was used among them. But since that time, the number of intemperate persons has greatly increased. In addition to the large quantities of whiskey, brought down the Ohio and Mississippi rivers, from the western States, the people are now in the habit of making from the sugar cane what they call *taffia*, a kind of liquor similar in its effects to New England rum. The priest remarked, that if we wished to see some of the evils of the intemperance, which prevails especially among the Americans, we might visit the grave yard at the mouth of the Bayou la Fourche, and we should find that a number of Americans were interred there, who had not lived out half their days; and who were killed by hard drinking. Not only have the Americans introduced great quantities of spirituous liquors, among the inhabitants of this southern country; but they are continually by their example leading them down to the pit. The boatmen, who pass up and down the river, are many of them vicious; and particularly addicted to intemperance. They have frequent intercourse with the inhabitants on the bank of the river, whose morals are seldom improved by this connexion.

The circulation of Religious Tracts, presenting the evils of intemperance, in the French and English languages, would, it is believed, be one of the best means that could be employed, to remedy the evil. At the present time, their case is every day becoming more alarming, and still not a hand is raised, not an effort is made to check the growing evil.

The Sabbath is generally profaned by the inhabitants of that country. They seem not to know, that the Lord hath said, *Remember the Sabbath day, to keep it holy.* Much of the vice and ignorance which prevails among them, is owing no doubt to their profanation of this sacred day. If Tracts could be put into their hands, presenting the awful sanctions of the holy Sabbath, and enjoining the observance of its sacred duties; in many instances we have reason to believe, a happy reformation would be effected.

Other Tracts, presenting the importance of giving moral and religious instruction to the rising generation, would be highly beneficial. —At present there are thousands of children, who grow up without being taught to read. Formerly, there was an influence exerted in this country, unfavourable to the education of the rising generation. At present, we believe, no considerable obstacles would present. It is principally owing to the negligence of the people, that schools are not established, and crowded with the youth of both sexes. Some of the Roman Catholics expressed an earnest desire, to provide their children with proper instruction. As soon as this disposition becomes general, they will be able to establish and support schools.

We believe, that Tracts on each of these subjects would be circulated by the Roman Catholic priests, and read with pleasure and profit by the people. A variety of moral and religious subjects might be treated of in the Tracts sent into this part of our country. Any thing of the kind will be novel and interesting to most of the inhabitants, and calculated to enlarge the minds, inform the understandings, and correct the practices of those who are our brethren, and have peculiar claims upon our friendly notice.—Certain gentlemen of our acquaintance in New Orleans, gave encouragement that they would translate some of the Tracts into the French language, if any means could be provided to defray the expense of printing them.

Yours most affectionately, &c.

XV. *Exertions on our return to New England.*

Andover, July 4, 1815.

Dear Sir,—As soon as the interesting business, on which we visited New Orleans, was accomplished, we hasted to return to our native land. The restoration of peace had opened the communication by sea. We thought it therefore not a duty to incur the fatigue and expense of travelling by land, from one extremity of the U. States almost to the other. The season was already far advanced. The weather in that latitude was excessively hot, and would be so on our whole journey. We concluded to return by sea. But then we wished, although we had no instructions to that effect, to visit as many of the southern cities as possible. Our object was, to endeavour to excite a spirit of liberality in the Atlantic States, and to turn the attention of the public, toward our western borders. We therefore waited a little for a passage to Savannah or Charleston. In the mean time Mr. Mills made an excursion of 150 miles into the Attakapas country, lying on the Gulf of Mexico, west of the Mississippi. Some of the French Testaments were to be distributed there. It was also very desirable that the western settlements of Louisiana should be explored. Mr. Mills had an interesting tour. But while he was gone, an opportunity presented of obtaining a passage to Charleston. Mr. Smith embraced it;—embarked on the eighth of April, and arrived safely in Charleston, after a tedious and somewhat hazardous voyage of twenty seven days. Here Mr. Smith had an opportunity of presenting the state of the western country, to a numerous audience collected for the purpose, from the different congregational and Presbyterian churches in the city. The deep interest manifested by the people on this occasion, is a pledge that they will yet do something, for the relief of their brethren in the west. In addition to the religious and charitable societies, that already existed in that city, exertions were making for the formation of a religious Tract Society.* The excellent Dr. Ramsey, it is said, was engaged in this business, on the very morning that he was assassinated. From Charleston, Mr. Smith sailed to Philadelphia.

Mr. Mills embarked at New Orleans, on the 30th of April, and arrived at Baltimore, on the 21st of May. During his stay there, he conversed with some of the managers of the Baltimore Bible Society, and obtained from them encouragement, that they would make a donation of Bibles, in favour of some portion of the western country.

We met again at Philadelphia. Soon afterwards we saw the managers of the Philadelphia Bible Society together; and reported to them the success of our agency in the distribution of the French Testaments. We gave them likewise the result of our inquiries, respecting the practicability of supplying the Spanish inhabitants of Louisiana, and of the adjacent countries, with the sacred Scriptures. At Philadelphia, we ascertained that the managers of the Bible Society, in consequence of representations we had made to them respecting the state of the western country, had voted a donation of 100 Bibles and 200 Testaments to the Indiana, Illinois, and Missouri Territories respectively. This generous donation has been forwarded accordingly.—We also addressed a note to Mrs. Ralston, President of the Female Bible Society, representing the state of New Orleans, with respect to a supply of the Scriptures. In consequence of which, the ladies who compose the board of managers, in that Society, determined to send 100 Bibles immediately to New Orleans.

At New Providence, N. J. Mr. Smith attended a meeting of the New Jersey Missionary Society. He gave the Board, at their request, the information of which we were possessed respecting the Cherokee Indians—and also urged upon their notice the Territories north of the Ohio, as missionary stations. This board is ready to support a missionary among the Cherokees, if a suitable person can

---

* Extract of a letter, from a friend in Charleston; dated, Aug. 25, 1815. " I have to convey to you, the gratifying intelligence, that since your departure from our city, we have succeeded in forming a Tract Society. Dr. Flinn is President. One hundred dollars have already been sent to Boston, to procure Tracts. So soon as they arrive, committees will be appointed to distribute them, in the most advantageous manner. The female members are to form part of the distributing committee, as generally speaking, they have more frequent opportunities of finding destitute objects."

be found. Some of the managers thought that they should soon send one into the north-western Territories.—At Newark, Mr. Smith had an opportunity of presenting the wants of the western people, to the citizens of that place. At the earnest request of Mr. Ward, secretary of the Newark Bible Society, he afterwards sketched down some of the principal facts, and addressed them to the Society; accompanied by an application, in behalf of Shawanee-town in the Illinois Territory, for a donation of Bibles. At New York we made a similar statement; and a similar application to the Bible Society of that city, for Bibles to be sent to Natchez. The success of the two last applications we have not yet learnt. While we were at New York, information was requested of us, by the managers of the Bible Society, respecting the best method of procedure in the distribution of their edition of French Bibles, which is now nearly completed. This request was readily complied with, and we suggested to them all the hints, that occurred to us as important on that subject. These Bibles, to the amount of 6,000 copies, are designed to be distributed, partly in the southern and western portions of the United States, and partly in Canada. At Hartford, Mr. Mills learnt that the Connecticut Bible Society had generously voted 500 Bibles, to its sister Society in Louisiana.

Thus, dear Sir, the streams of christian charity are beginning to flow into that thirsty, barren land, where no water is. Would to God they might continue and increase, until every corner and every heart shall be refreshed with the water of life.*

———

We have now, dear Sir, given you a brief account of our tour—of our exertions, and of the success with which the Lord has been pleased to favour us, in advancing the kingdom of our Redeemer. We have presented you with some sketches, of the moral and religious state of the country, through which we have passed.—In reviewing the whole, we feel compelled to call upon our own souls, and to call upon the patrons of the mission, to bless the Lord. Surely goodness and mercy have followed us all the way. On a journey of more than six thousand miles, and passing through a great variety of climates—in perils in the city, in perils in the wilderness, in perils on the rivers, and in perils on the sea—the Lord has preserved us.— Neither can we forbear to express our obligations to our dear christian friends in the western country. We were strangers and they took us in. From many we received pecuniary aid,† besides other important services; while the kind attentions and christian fellowship of others alleviated our labours and comforted our hearts.

In return for these favours, we have felt compelled to do what we could for them. Ever since we came back to this land of christian privileges, we have been endeavouring to arouse the attention of the

* See Appendix, L.
† See Appendix, M.

public, and to direct it towards the west. These exertions have been stimulated by a deep conviction of the deplorable state of that country. Never will the impression be erased from our hearts, that has been made by beholding those scenes of wide-spreading desolation. The whole country, from Lake Erie to the gulf of Mexico, is as the valley of the shadow of death. Darkness rests upon it. Only here and there, a few rays of gospel light pierce through the awful gloom. This vast country contains more than a million of inhabitants. Their number is every year increased, by a mighty flood of emigration Soon they will be as the sands on the sea shore for multitude. Yet there are at present only a little more than one hundred Presbyterian or Congregational ministers in it. Were these ministers equally distributed throughout the country; there would be only one to every ten thousand people. But now there are districts of country, containing from twenty to fifty thousand inhabitants, entirely destitute. *And how shall they hear without a preacher?*

From the estimates made in the preceding pages, it appears that *seventy six thousand families,* are destitute of the sacred volume, in this portion of our country. These estimates are not ungrounded and exaggerated conjectures. They are the result of much inquiry, and patient examination. It is our sober conviction, that at least 76,000 Bibles are necessary for the supply of the destitute. And the number is every year increasing. Most of those who emigrate from the older States are poor: there are many young men who go into that country, and are married afterwards—and never have an opportunity of supplying their families with Bibles. The number of Bibles, sent there by all the Societies in the United States, is by no means as great, as the yearly increase of the destitute. The original number still remains unsupplied. When we entered on the mission, we applied in person to the oldest and wealthiest of these institutions, for Bibles to distribute in the western country: but we could only obtain one solitary donation. The existing Societies have not yet been able to supply the demand, in their own immediate vicinity. Some mightier effort must be made. Their scattered and feeble exertions, are by no means adequate to the accomplishment of the object. It is thought by judicious people, that *half a million of Bibles* are necessary, for the supply of the destitute in the United States. It is a foul blot on our national character. Christian America must arise and wipe it away.—The existing Societies are not able to do it. They want union;—they want co-operation;—they want resources. If a National Institution cannot be formed, application ought to be made to the British and Foreign Bible Society for aid.

Yours in the bonds of christian affection,
SAMUEL J. MILLS.
DANIEL SMITH.

APPENDIX.

A.

M<small>R</small>. Wright's account of the conversion of his profane neighbour is worthy of being given at length, as an encouragement to the friends of Bible Societies.

As Mr. Wright was out one day, on one of his parochial visits, he called at a place, where a number of people were assembled at a raising. While he was conversing with some of them, he mentioned that he had Bibles in his hands for distribution. There was a man standing by, who had been noted for impiety and profanity. This man, hearing Mr. W. observe, that he had Bibles to give away, felt for the first time a strong, and to him, unaccountable desire, to possess one. He came forward and asked Mr. W. if he would give him a Bible. Mr. W. told him he would, if he would read it. During the conversation the man made use of some profane expression. The good clergyman told him, that he wished him to call and get a Bible; and added, that he hoped it would produce an alteration in his conduct and *conversation*. The man attempted to apologize for his profanity, and engaged to call for the Bible. Some people thought, that charity might be better bestowed, than in giving the Bible to such a profane sinner. But the next day he called at Mr. Wright's house ; and he gave him a Bible, enjoining it upon him to read it. He said that he had been married more than thirteen years, and had never had a Bible in the house; and that he had not read a chapter, since he was a school-boy. He promised however that he would peruse it.

The very next Sabbath, this man was seen at the house of God. He afterwards confessed that he had not heard a sermon before, for eight or ten years. During the intermission, Mr. W. spoke with him, and asked if he had been reading his Bible. He answered, that he had read in it some ; and that what he had read, made him feel very uncomfortable. He added, that if what he read in that book was true, he feared that his case was hopeless. He thought he must stop reading it, and put it out of his house. Mr. W. reminded him of his promise to read the Bible, when he received it ; and told him he ought to examine and see whether it was true. The man concluded that he would go home, and read his Bible farther. The next Sabbath he was at meeting again, and gave very strict attention.

From the time that this man received the Bible, his mind became more and more impressed. His countenance and deportment were affected. His wife and daughter observed the change, and were apprehensive that he would become crazy. They attributed the alteration in him, to his reading the Bible, and beset him to put it out of the house. He refused to comply, and continued to read. After a few weeks, he told his family, that it would not do to live so : he must commence family worship. His wife was not pleased with this; but she concluded, that perhaps it might relieve his mind ; and at length consented. He began to pray with his family. He was constant at the house of God, and gave evidence of genuine piety. Now he invokes a blessing on those who support Bible Societies. He reads his Bible—sheds tears of joy—bursts into a song, and sings surprising grace.

Mr. W. informed us, when we were with him, that this man's daughter was in deep distress on account of her sins.

Ye, who have Bibles enough and to spare, will ye not give one ? Ye stewards of the Most high, will ye not give any thing, to send the Bible unto hundreds and thousands of such families ?

B.

The leading characters of the Methodist Society are very active, in supplying the western country with religious books. The books they furnish are principally the following :—Wesley's and Fletcher's works—Wesley's notes on the New Testament—Methodist Book of Discipline—Methodist Hymn Book, &c. All these are directly calculated to promote the interests of their own Society. A few Bibles are likewise furnished. It is generally said in the western country, that the members of that connexion are expected to purchase all their books of the preachers and other agents of the Society ;—and that the Society will take care to furnish them with all that are needful. The impression seems also to be general, that the books are sold very low —even at cost. In the Mississippi Territory, Bibles, of the pocket edition, with plain binding, are sold at *three dollars;* with elegant binding, at *four.*

This energetic Society sends out an immense quantity of these books. We found them almost every where. In the possession of the obscurest families, we often found a number of volumes. There had been sent into the Illinois Territory, as we were informed by a respectable Methodist gentlemen, seventeen hundred dollars' worth of their books. These were designed to supply the western part of that Territory; and the avails of the sales, as we understood, were to be laid out in furnishing more books. In the interior of the Mississippi Territory, Mr. Smith found three or four boxes of these same books deposited at one house for sale. If this Society bestows a proportionate attention on the other Territories and States, the amount of books sent annually into the western country, must be very great. It puts to the blush all the other charitable institutions in the United States.

7

C.

Extract from Mr. Smith's journal, dated,
Shawanee-town, Oct. 27, 1814.

My heart is pained at the sight of this land of darkness, and the shadow of death. When we first entered this Territory, at the house of the ferryman on the Wabash, we found two families who had no Bible. The father of one of the families, an elderly man, said he never had a Bible in his house. He had been poor, and often was unable to purchase. But he had often applied at the stores in Shawanee-town, to buy a Bible; but could not find any. Sometimes he was contemptuously asked, What he wanted of a Bible ? and What good that book would do him ? But for my part, said he with strong emotion, if I had one, I would not exchange it for any other book;— for the Bible I believe is the *greatest book* in the world. We told him, that if he would apply again at Shawanee-town, he should have a Bible. We had sent fifty there for distribution.

D.

Extract of a letter, from Rev. Samuel F. Scott.
" *Vincennes, (Ind. Ter.) Jan. 25, 1815.*

" *Rev. and dear Sir,*—Agreeably to the appointment, when you left Vincennes, the citizens met and formed themselves into a Society, for the purpose of circulating the sacred Scriptures. The name of the Society is " The Vincennes Bible Society." The managers are fifteen in number. Judge Benjamin Parke is President. The committee of correspondence consists of four : viz. Doctor Jacob Kuykendall, Rev. Isaac M'Koy, Daniel M'Clure, Esq., and Samuel F. Scott. Our subscription is about two hundred dollars, and increasing. Our Society has already had a good effect. I am yours,
" S. F. SCOTT."

E.

Extract of a letter, from his Excellency Thomas Posey.
" *Jeffersonville, (Ind. Ter.) Jan. 27, 1815.*

" *Reverend and esteemed Messrs. Mills and Smith,*—Agreeably to my promise, I can inform you, that the Bible Society, which we have made some progress in exertions to establish, is not yet matured. At New Albany and this village, there are subscribed about two hundred dollars. Judge James Scott informs me, that at Charlestown the subscription is small—does not say to what amount, but expects, that the people, when they come to understand the true principles of the Society, will subscribe liberally.....As soon as the winter breaks, notice will be given to the subscribers to attend another meeting. If my health is restored sufficiently, I will attend it. I feel considerably interested in having the Society perfected as speedily as possible.—

I have given out the twenty five Bibles you left with me.....I have given away nearly all the pamphlets, &c.

"I am very respectfully your friend,

"T. POSEY."

At New Albany, we witnessed the distribution of fifty Bibles, sent there by the Newark Auxiliary Bible Society. The eagerness of the people to obtain copies was astonishing. Mr. Nathaniel Scribner, the gentleman to whose care they were committed had more applications for Bibles than he could supply. Two young men, having heard of the circumstance, came on the Sabbath—a stormy and uncomfortable day, twenty miles, to obtain Bibles. When they received them, they placed them in their bosom. They were induced to tarry and hear a sermon; and then went home in the night, rejoicing that they had obtained such a treasure. In a few days the Bibles were all gone; and Mr. Scribner said he could immediately distribute a hundred more, if he had them.

F.

Extract of a letter, from Stephen Hempsted Esq. to Mr. Smith.

"*St. Louis, (Missouri Ter.) June* 6, 1815.

"*Respected friend,*—I have nothing that I can communicate to you, in respect to our destitute situation, more than you have seen, and been informed of, when you visited St. Louis. There has not a clergyman of any class visited these parts, since you were here, to my knowledge.....I have not the least doubt, that a man of good moral character, good talents and education, would be cordially received and well provided for, by the people,—and would do much good, in establishing correct principles and forming churches here. The time is not yet come for us to receive so great a blessing, as to have the gospel stately preached, and the ordinances administered to us. God's time is the best time. He will send by whom he will the blessings he designs, for any church or people;—and will be sought unto, for all the blessings we desire. *Brethren, pray for us;* that we may not be impatient, but wait God's time, to bestow these blessings on this part of our land........Don't forget our destitute situation, when you make report to the Society.

"Yours in christian affection and esteem,

"STEPHEN HEMPSTED."

"P. S. *June* 13. The box of Bibles and Testaments has just arrived safe. I open my letter to inform you."

G.

Extract of a letter, from Rev. James M'Gready to Mr. Mills.

"*Red Banks, Henderson County, (Ken.) April* 27, 1815.

"*Reverend and dear Sir,*—I received your letter dated the 11th of

January, with the Religious Tracts, which you sent to me for distribution. I have used every possible exertion in the distribution of the Tracts, where I hoped they would have the desired effect.—I have found them universally received with gratitude, in every place where I have presented them; and I have generally seen the families where they are presented, all attention to them, and every person reading them with seriousness and solemnity. I am extremely pleased with the plan, and I sincerely believe that I could distribute a thousand of them to advantage; and I must think, if persevered in, it will be a blessed means of promoting the salvation and immortal interests of many; especially in a country like ours, where there are hundreds of precious souls, bound for the eternal world, that cannot be persuaded to attend the public preaching of the gospel. When I received your letter, I designed to carry it to the spring meeting of our Presbytery, and to have made proposals, for the formation of a Religious Tract Society in our own bounds. But being prevented from attending, by reason of the excessive high waters, nothing has been done in that business yet. But during the summer, I shall use every exertion in my power to effect it, and shall write to you again on the subject, towards the fall.

" If some Religious Tracts were in my possession, showing the vanity and soul-destroying nature of giddy balls and vain amusements —some treating of the importance of secret prayer—some of the danger of quenching convictions—some giving an account of extraordinary conversions—such, I think, I could distribute to advantage.

" You desire me to give you some information of the wants of the people in this country, with respect to the Holy Scriptures, and whether a gratuitous distribution of them here would answer a valuable purpose. In answer to this I would say, There are multitudes in the motley, mixed population of this western country, that have not a Bible in their houses, and probably never had. There are many people here, and people of property too—and what the world call, people of respectability, that know no more of the contents of the Bible, than the Shawanees or Choctaws do. I have asked many of this description, whether they believe the truth of the Scriptures or not. I have frequently received such answers as these : ' I do not know, it is probable they are true, but I have never thought about it—indeed I have never read the Bible much—I never had one.'

" In the bounds of this County, where I spend my labours, a pious lady informed me that a lady of her acquaintance, the wife of a deist, was under very serious impressions; and solemnly concerned about her eternal state—that she had an intense desire to read the Bible, but there was no Bible in her house, and that her husband would not get one for her—that all her entreaties to him on that subject were in vain. I procured a Bible for her. This woman, some time after, obtained a blessed hope of salvation, through the mediation and atonement of Jesus Christ. And some months after, she died happy, rejoicing in the prospect of a glorious immortality.

" Upon a certain day, I called at a house where I had business. The lady and her children being alone, I asked her some solemn questions about the state of her soul, and found by her answers, that she had a feeling sense of her lost, undone state. She lamented her situation—her chance for attending public preaching was bad. Her husband was a deist. He looked upon religion as foolishness, and was a hindrance to her attending. She lamented her ignorance, and told me that her parents had neglected her education. Yet she could read the New Testament, but could not get one. She had times without number entreated her husband to get her a Testament; but he would not. I proposed to furnish her with one; and she appeared much rejoiced.* From these and similar circumstances, I am confident, that Bibles and Testaments could be distributed to advantage.

" I am, with respect, your sincere friend and brother
in the gospel of Christ,
" JAMES M'GREADY."

Extract of a letter, from the Rev. William Dickey, to Mr. Mills.

" *Salem, Livingston County,* (*Ken.*) *April* 1, 1815.

" *Dear Sir,*—Some weeks ago, I was at the mouth of Cumberland river, where I received a bundle of Religious Tracts, and a letter from you, informing me from whence they came, and what to do with them. I thank you, Sir—The first bundle of Religious Tracts I ever saw. I read them eagerly, and was glad to have it in my power, to give away a present, so suitable, and so acceptable, to many a destitute family. I directed those who received them, to read them over and over, and then hand them to their neighbours. Be assured, Sir, they have excited considerable interest among all classes. Religious Tracts have been much desired by us, ever since we heard of Societies of this kind. But we were never, until now, able to appreciate their worth. That so many numbers, and 6000 of each, should be printed for gratuitous distribution, astonishes our people. They say, *It is the Lord's doing, and marvellous in our eyes.*

" You desire to know the probable number of poor, destitute families, in this vicinity, who might wish to be possessed of the sacred Scriptures. Dear Sir, I see, or think I see, another blessing, in the bosom of this request. I dare not hazard a conjecture, in answer to your inquiry. But perhaps you will meet your object, when I tell you, that we have lately distributed twenty eight Bibles, which we received from the Kentucky Bible Society; and that this number, instead of supplying the destitute among and around us, has only brought them into view.

" I am, dear stranger, with sentiments of gratitude,
your obedient friend,
" WILLIAM DICKEY."

---

* We wish here to meet an objection, sometimes urged against the gratuitous distribution of the Scriptures. The objection is, that if a man is able to purchase a Bible, but is too regardless of religion to do it, he will derive no profit from it, if it is presented to him. This we do not grant; and as a proof of the contrary, we refer to Mr. Wright's account. [Appendix, A.] But if the father of a family be not profited, by the gift of a Bible; the wife, or the children, may be made wise unto salvation. In the two instances related by Mr. M'Gready, who would refuse to give a Bible?

54

From Mr. William Harris, with whom we became acquainted at New Madrid, on the bank of the Mississippi, we received a letter, dated at St. Genevieve, March 26, 1815, the substance of which is as follows.

My dear Friend,

I left New Madrid on the 10th of February. The English Bibles and French Testaments, which you left there, were received with much joy. The Tracts were much sought after, and were lent from one to another. The Tracts are very necessary, in order to excite attention; and to answer that question which sometimes occurs, viz. *What shall I do to be saved.* As I am a pedlar in this country, I have an opportunity of learning the character of the people. Many of them are exceedingly debased. Some of those, deemed the most respectable, are much addicted to vice. Gambling, intemperance, and profane swearing are very common. The condition of females is sadly degraded. In many parts of the country, they are obliged to perform a considerable proportion of masculine labour; while their husbands are unprofitably roving with their guns. Tracts, on a variety of moral and religious subjects, would doubtless be the means of strengthening the hands of the few, who are virtuously disposed; particularly those, which present the evils of intemperance, gambling, and profane swearing. I inclose in my letter to you a twenty dollar bill, for the use of the New England Tract Society. If it be proper, you may record me as a member of the Society. If it be not proper, my object will be answered, by the appropriation of the twenty dollars for the circulation of those excellent Tracts.

I am, with high considerations of esteem,
your obliged friend and humble servant,
WILLIAM HARRIS.

H.

Copy of a letter, from the Rev. Charles Coffin of Tennessee, to the Rev. Abel Flint.

Green County, June 7, 1815.

" *Rev. Sir,*—It is with great pleasure we have heard of the present revival of religion in Yale College. A similar display of divine grace in Princeton College is, also, a matter of great thankfulness. When God casts the salt into the largest fountains of science in our land, streams must issue which will gladden his people. Dear Sir, we are here in a wilderness;—I had almost said, in a dry and thirsty land, where no water is. The Presbyterian ministers here are as nothing to the demand of the population. The fields are white for the harvest; but what shall be done for labourers? We have received intimations that a Missionary Society in Connecticut, of which you are a member, may have it in their power to send one or two missionaries. O, Sir, if they can, do see that it is done. The common cause might be greatly advanced by such a step. The call for preaching in our vacant churches and destitute settlements is universally great. Should your missionaries be directed to consult with the Trustees of the East Tennessee Missionary Society, as to their field of labour, it might favour their usefulness. We hope the showers of divine grace are not to pass by this western part of our country. But means must be in proportionable operation, before we can look for an extensive blessing. You will perceive by the last census that the population of East Tennessee is about 100,000. But only seven or eight Presbyterian ministers are ordained among them, and one or two candidates coming forward. Our hands might be much strengthened and our hearts encouraged by any aid Connecticut may be able to send us. We fear less injury to the cause of religion here from sectarianism, wild and irregular as it often is, than from irreligion, ignorance and stupidity. Well qualified Missionaries would be sure to gain attention, from the various denominations among the people. If it should be necessary, our Missionary Society would contribute to their support from what is now in our scanty funds. Hereafter, perhaps, our pecuniary ability will be greater.

"I should have written at much greater length, and given a broader and fuller view of this subject, but the pressure of indispensable duties at this time, has prevented.

"Relying on your zeal to build up the kingdom of our dear Redeemer, I remain with respect and affection your unworthy brother,
"CHARLES COFFIN."

Copy of a letter from the Rev. Isaac Anderson of the State of Tennessee, to the Rev. Abel Flint, Secretary of the Missionary Society of Connecticut.

"*East Tennessee, Blount County, Maryville, May 11, 1815.*"

"*Rev. Sir,*—It has been suggested to me that there is a probability that the Missionary Society, of which you are Secretary, could send us one, or perhaps two Missionaries. If you can, it will be an inestimable blessing.—We have a Society called the 'East Tennessee Missionary Society;' the object of which is to spread the knowledge of Christ, in destitute places in East Tennessee, by the distribution of Bibles and Religious Tracts, and by sending preachers. We have no preachers. There are eighteen counties in East Tennessee; and there is not more than 3000 souls out of a population of 100,000, that have any opportunity to hear the gospel, except from illiterate men, many of whom cannot even read the Scriptures. How gloomy the picture! But, Sir, you can have no conception of it unless you were here. *Perhaps one fourth of our population has not a Bible;* and hundreds of them are taught that it is not very essential. A more needy field of missionary labours can hardly exist.

"Can your Society send us a missionary and support him, (though we would if we could, and will do all we can,) to labour under the direction of our Society as to time and place? How thankfully should we receive him! Present our case to your Society. Although this is a solicitation of an individual, yet I know I speak the mind of the Society, and were they all here I believe they would sign this letter.
"Your brother in the gospel of Christ.
"ISAAC ANDERSON."

I.

Extract of a letter, from Rev. William R. Gould.

"*Gallipolis, Gallia County, (Ohio,) June 12, 1815.*

"*Beloved Brother,*—It rejoices me, that I have had the privilege of being a small partaker in the work of which you are a principal. You sent ten French Testaments to this place, from Shippingport, [Falls of Ohio,] Jan. 3, 1815.—It was an offering of sweet smelling savour. It fell to my happy lot to distribute them. I carried them to the houses of our French neighbours, and spread the word of life before them. I explained the object and wishes of the benevolent Bible Society, which sent them the Testaments; presented some evidences of its divine original; showed its desirableness—its adaptedness to our wants, and urged the necessity of reading it, and of obeying its precepts. In almost every instance, it was received with expressions, and most evident tokens of gratitude. In one instance, on presenting a Testament, the affecting reply was, "Oh, Sir, this is too much." And again—to a native of St. Domingo, who did not before know what the Bible was. "It is just what I want—I thank you." I have found places for them all. May God accompany them with his blessing, and reward the benevolent donors."

"Yours in the Lord,
"WILLIAM R. GOULD."

Extract of a letter, from Mr. D. Dufour, translated from the French.

"*Vevay, Swisserland County, (Ind. Ter.) June 20, 1815.*

"*Mr. S. J. Mills, Sir,*—In the beginning of May, I received your very acceptable letter, dated January 3, 1815, with ten copies of the French New Testament, printed by the Philadelphia Bible Society. The reception of the Testaments has afforded real pleasure, both to me, and the Swiss families, among whom I have distributed them."

[Mr. Dufour regrets, to use his own expression, ' that a book so sacred as the New Testament had not been printed with greater care.' He had noticed some typographical errors; and also that the binder had so folded the leaves in some of the copies, that some of the words, and even lines, were cut off.*]

"But notwithstanding these defects, this valuable present has been received among us with much joy; and all the families, which have received copies, have charged me to present to you their cordial salutations, and sincere thanks. While I express their sentiments of

* We think the remarks of Mr. D. are worthy the serious consideration of the managers of Bible Societies. Economy has perhaps been too much consulted heretofore, by those who have printed Bibles and Testaments for gratuitous distribution. The Directors of the British and Foreign Bible Society have thought it best to recommend the Bibles and Testaments circulated by them, by the superior style in which they are executed. As soon as the Religious public in this country shall feel on this subject, as its importance demands; our societies will not want for resources, to enable them to follow such an example.

gratitude, I pray you, my dear Mr. Mills, to accept my own in particular; and to present the same, in the name of us all, to the respectable Philadelphia Bible Society.

"With sincere respect and fraternal affection,

"D. Dufour."

A brief account of this settlement may be interesting to the reader. It was commenced in 1803 by three families, originally from the Canton de Vaud, near the Geneva Lake in Switzerland. In the course of a few years, it was increased by eight or ten families from Switzerland. In 1812 there were between seventy and eighty souls in the place. Since that time, the settlement has been increasing. The principal object of these people is the cultivation of vineyards. They have about fifty acres planted with the vines, which already begin to be productive. They have made, in the course of a year, more than 4000 gallons of wine. By some the wine is esteemed equal to the claret of Bordeaux. They are honest and industrious; and were in the habit of meeting together on the Sabbath, for religious worship. They are, as far as we could learn, Calvinistic in their religious sentiments. Vevay is about 70 miles below Cincinnati, and 8 above the mouth of the Kentucky river.

K.

Report of the Louisiana Bible Society.

The board of managers of the Louisiana Bible Society, respectfully offer the following Report relative to the progress made by the Society since its institution, [29th of March, 1813.]

The Bibles (in English) and the New Testaments (in French) which we have hitherto circulated, are the donations of other sister Societies.

From the New York Bible Society was received, in the summer of 1813, a donation of 150 English Bibles, through the hands of the Rev. Messrs. Schermerhorn and Mills. From the Massachusetts Bible Society was received, in the month of February, 1815, a donation of 140 English Bibles, sent on by the Rev. Messrs. Mills and Smith, visiting this country as *missionaries.* By the same gentlemen, the Philadelphia Bible Society has forwarded 3,000 French New Testaments, a part of the edition of 5,000, which that Society, aided by sister Societies, and different individuals, has printed for gratuitous distribution among the French of the State of Louisiana, and the Territories of Missouri and Illinois.

From the British and Foreign Bible Society, the parent of a thousand like institutions, existing in Europe and America, we have to acknowledge a generous donation of 100l. sterling; one among many other instances of the very extended and benevolent views of that most noble institution of modern times.

Of the English Bibles there have been distributed,

64 among 300 British prisoners in the public prison at New Orleans.

30 among 300 patients of the United States hospital, (of whom 180 were British prisoners.)

8

31 among 240 sick in hospitals of the Kentucky militia.
31 among 265 sick in hospitals of the Tennessee militia.
34 among 360 sick in hospitals of the Louisiana militia.
 8 among 50 sick in the United States navy hospital.
36 among the heads of American families in the county of Attaka-
    pas.
12 among the heads of American families on the Amite and Comite
    rivers, Florida.
44 to individuals at New Orleans.
——
290 in the whole, and leaving the Society without a single Bible in
    English, at a time too in which numerous applications are mak-
    ing for them.

Of 3000 *copies of the French New Testament received in this city,
there have been distributed,*

2000 among the inhabitants of New Orleans and its environs.
112 have been sent for distribution to the county of Natchitoches.
 42 for the county of Rapides.
200 to the county of Attakapas.
800 copies of the French New Testament have been forwarded by
    the Philadelphia Bible Society, and committed to the care of
    different gentlemen residing on the river between this city and
    Natchez, for gratuitous distribution among the inhabitants of
    their vicinity.

The want of Bibles in Louisiana has been extreme; and it will yet
require a very considerable number to supply in an adequate manner
the families which are destitute of the word of God. Had three thousand English Bibles and as many New Testaments been in the hands
of the managers at the beginning of the past winter, they could have
been distributed in this city with the greatest facility, and it is believed with much advantage; so good an opportunity will not probably occur for some time to come. Our regular troops and militia then
here were remarkably destitute of the scriptures.

It was very unusual to find any portion of the sacred volume among
our soldiers; and in many instances there were found an hundred sick
assembled in a hospital, without having among them one Bible or
New Testament.

Some of the Tennessee militia, when passing through Nashville on
their way to New Orleans, had inquired in vain for a Bible; not one
was to be found for sale; and in the month of December last a similar inquiry was fruitlessly made in this city by a gentleman from the
Amite—*nor is there at this moment a Bible to be purchased in a bookstore in the city of New Orleans.*

The inhabitants of Florida, who are principally Americans, are
generally without the Scriptures; so are the other Americans, for
the most part, throughout the state. It has been supposed, and it is
believed with the strictest correctness, that before the transmission of
a few French Bibles to New Orleans by the British and Foreign Bible Society, in the year 1813, there were not *ten* among the French
inhabitants of Louisiana.

The manner in which the Scriptures have been received by those to whom they have been distributed, is highly gratifying, and encourages the belief that the labours of those who have united in this work will not be lost.

The Tennessee and Kentucky troops received the Bibles with no ordinary willingness—it seemed to be received by many of them as " *a pearl of great price.*"

As there were not Bibles sufficient to supply even the sick in hospitals, who are anxious to receive them, it was not uncommon to see one reading aloud to several around; and at other times two or three lying on the floor together would be attempting to read in the same book at the same time. Some of those, who had received Bibles, declared their intention to carry them home with them on foot 800 or 1000 miles; and rather than not carry them they said they would throw away part of their baggage.

The French have received the New Testament with much satisfaction. It is possible that some have asked for it from curiosity; but very many have done so from a wish to *search the scriptures,* which numbers declared they had never seen before. It must give pleasure to every philanthropic mind to learn that the rising generation in this city, heretofore almost destitute of any book of instruction, has now a class book used throughout our schools—that those children whose parents were unable from the exorbitant price of school books and the pressure of the war to furnish them, have now a book " which hath God for its author, salvation for its end, and truth, without any mixture of error, for its matter."

Although the three thousand copies of the New Testament in French had been received by the president of the society about the middle of December last, owing to the disturbed situation of the country, at that time invaded, none of them were distributed until about the 10th of February—after a few persons had received the New Testament, and it had become generally known, that there were more in the hands of one of the managers, who had been appointed to make the gratuitous distribution of the whole number designed for the city, the applications were more frequent than could be supplied —a large crowd of some hundreds of people of all colours and ranks, was formed before the house, and became literally clamorous to have " *a book,*" a word which was often vociferated in French by fifty voices at once.

Such an assembly, for such a purpose, never before witnessed in Louisiana, presented to the beholder many affecting scenes—the young and the old, the rich and the poor, as if alike conscious of their wants, pressed forward with outstretched hands, to receive the valuable gift—a child not more than five or six years of age, was borne in the arms of its mother, a woman of colour, pressing through the crowd as one of the canditates for a treasure which she seemed justly to estimate; the silence and attention exhibited by the bystanders was immediately rewarded by hearing this infant read in an intelligent manner the story related in Mark x. 13, 16, [*And they brought young children to him, that he should touch them; and his disciples rebuked those that brought them. But when Jesus saw it, he was much displeased, and said unto them, Suffer the little children to come unto me, and forbid them not : for of such is the kingdom of God. Verily I say unto you, Whosoever shall not receive the kingdom of God as a little child, he shall not enter therein. And he took them up in his arms, put his hands upon them, and blessed them,]* rendered doubly interesting by the incidents.

As all who presented themselves for a French New Testament were asked if they could read, and if any doubts existed, were put to the trial : an aged black woman, being asked the usual question, and requested to prove the fact, answered that she could not without her spectacles, which she had not with her; but unwilling to depart until the object of her wishes had been obtained, she renewed her application, and observed to the distributor, " if I get a book by a falsehood it will not be deceiving you, but God." Many persons who could not read themselves, wished the New Testament for their children, who, they said, would read it for them.

The managers have received the hearty co-operation of many individuals in distributing the French New Testament. The reverend father Antonio de Sedilla, the curate of the parish, has taken an active part in aiding the circulation of the New Testament among the Catholics ; the countenance given by him to the views of the Society is of the highest importance, from the great influence which he has among his parishoners. We acknowledge likewise with pleasure the aid of several gentlemen; nor in any instance has assistance been refused.

The British prisoners, to whom a portion of the English Bibles were distributed, manifested the sincerest joy and gratitude; most of them had been supplied with Bibles or Testaments previous to their embarkation for this country; and some (as appeared by a printed notification in the Testaments) by the Naval Bible Association, established as long ago as 1780, but having left their heavy baggage, at their camp on the 8th of January, the day on which a general assault was made on the lines near this city, they became destitute when made prisoners.

During the past year this Society has received many interesting reports from the numerous Bible Societies now established in the United States; the information contained in them is in a high degree gratifying and encouraging to the promoters of these associations. Some few extracts from these valuable communications will be found in the Appendix. The committee, however, cannot omit on this occasion earnestly to recommend the perusal of such reports; they afford the best views of the design, the utility and progress of these Societies.

Before concluding this Report the committee beg leave to call upon the Society for a cordial union in the vigorous prosecution of diffusing the light of " the glorious gospel of the blessed God."

The gospel is entrusted to us, not for our own sakes only, but for the benefit of the world. We receive, that we may communicate.— Religion, like other blessings, is to be diffused by human agency and human benevolence. It has flowed to us through the zeal and labour of those who have gone before us; and we are bound to repay the debt by spreading it around us, and transmitting it unimpaired to succeeding ages. To this most worthy cause of God and holiness, of human happiness and virtue, a cause which can never fail, which is destined to survive the schemes of statesmen, and the trophies of conquerors, let us attach ourselves with a disinterested and persevering zeal, which will prove us followers of him who lived and died to enlighten and redeem mankind.

Great and magnificent is the undertaking in which we are engaged; great too are the consequences which we may rationally hope will be their result. Let no minor difficulties impede our progress; rather let them animate our exertions and quicken our pace. The hundredth part of the zeal and humanity of a Howard, exerted by each of us, would convey the Bible to the most secluded mansion in our country—would put into the hands of the widow, the 'fatherless, and the afflicted, the words of everlasting consolation. A zeal like his pervading our institutions, would print the word of God in every language of the earth, and give to every son of Adam, "the scriptures, which are able to make wise unto salvation, through faith which is in Christ Jesus." Let no objections of infidels, or pretended friends, make us hesitate or swerve from the way; though the Bible alone has not yet converted whole nations, it may be the first step in the grand undertaking: it may prepare the way for missionaries; and though, in countries denominated christian, much ignorance and vice may remain after the Bible has been generally distributed, no one can say that it may not have extirpated much which would have taken root, had no exertions been made to repress them. "The operation of the Bible is necessarily gradual and noiseless—its province is the heart, and its best fruits are those mild and humble virtues, which ask no notice but from the eye of God. It is enough to know that we have sown the good seed of divine truth, and we may leave it with confidence to Him, whose grace descends as the dew, and who has promised that the desert and solitary place shall blossom as the rose."

ALFRED HENNEN, *Secretary.*

New Orleans, April 25.

Since this report was written, a box containing thirty Bibles in French, and twelve New Testaments in Spanish, printed and bound in an elegant manner by the British and Foreign Bible Society, have been forwarded to the president of the Society—a present truly valuable.

L

Bibles, which are sent into the western States or Territories for distribution, may for the present be directed to the care of the following gentlemen:—Rev. Samuel P. Robbins, Corresp. Secretary of the Ohio Bible Society, Marietta, Ohio. Mr. Nathaniel Burrows, Lexington, Kentucky. His Excellency Thomas Posey, Jeffersonville, Indiana Territory. Mr. Joel Scribner, New Albany, Indiana Territory. Mr. Joseph M. Street, Shawanee-town, Illinois Territory. Stephen Hempsted Esq. St. Louis, Missouri Territory. Rev. Charles Coffin, D. D. President of Greenville College, East Tennessee. Rev.

Samuel Hodge, Summer County, near Nashville, West Tennessee. John Henderson Esq. Natchez, Mississippi Territory. Alfred Hennen Esq. Secretary of the Louisiana Bible Society, New Orleans.

M.

ACCOUNT OF RECEIPTS AND EXPENDITURES.

1814.	MISSION,		Dr.
July 29.	To cash paid for waggon and harness	-	$119 20
Aug. 5.	To expenses from Litchfield to Philadelphia 180 miles	-	20 04
15.	To expenses at Philadelphia, 10 days	-	32 28
30.	To expenses from Philadelphia to Pittsburgh 280 miles	-	31 70
Sept. 18.	To expenses from Pittsburgh to Marietta 180 m.		23 54
Oct. 4.	To expenses from Marietta to Cincinnati, 218 miles distance travelled	-	17 64
Nov. 8.	To expenses from Cincinnati to St. Louis, 497 miles distance travelled	-	28 50
29.	To expenses from St. Louis to Louisville, 392 miles distance travelled	-	23 62
Dec. 15.	To expenses from Louisville to Lexington, and back, 160 miles	-	23 12
1815.	To necessaries for the passage from Louisville		
Jan. 4.	to Natchez	-	17 62
Feb. 7.	To expense of passage from Louisville to Natchez, 1,239 miles in thirty two days	-	64 00
Mar. 10.	To expenses from Natchez to New Orleans, 150 miles by land; 300 miles by water	-	31 72
April 30.	To expenses at New Orleans, Mr. Smith's board, &c.	54 74	
	Mr. Mills's expenses at Attakapas	18 50	
	Mr. Mills's board	77 62	
			150 86
May 29.	To expenses from New Orleans to Philadelphia.——Mr. Smith's passage to Charleston	50 25	
	Mr. Smith's passage to Philadelphia	35 37	
	Mr. Mills's passage to Baltimore	91 25	
	Mr. Mills's passage to Philadelphia	11 99	
			188 86
June 19.	To expenses from Philadelphia to Boston.		
	Mr. Mills's bills	41 23	
	Mr. Smith's bills	38 45	
			79 68

Amount carried up $852, 38

Amount brought up		$852 38

June 19. To Mr. Smith's private expenses, includ-
ing clothes, equipage, &c. -   -   161 82
To Mr. Mills's private expenses including
clothes, equipage, &c. estimated at   161 82
To loss on the sale of Mr. Smith's horse   50 00
To loss on Mr. Mills's horse, (say)   50 00

                    423 64

Amount of money paid out $1276 02
From which deduct cash received for
waggon sold at Natchez   -   148 00
Price of buffaloe robe, Atlas, &c.   -   11 50

                    159 50

Amount of expense corrected $1116 52

1814. MISSION,   Cr.

July 29. By cash from Massachusetts Missionary Society   400 00
Aug. 14. Do. Philadelphia Bible Society   200 00
Sep. 10. Do. Massachusetts Missionary Society
in a letter from Mr. Evarts   -   -   -   10 00
1815. By cash from the Mass. Miss. Soc. on a draught
Mar. 30. on Mr. Turo of New Orleans, from H. Gray   200 00
June 2. By cash from Philadelphia Bible Society   400 00
3.   Do. Philadelphia Missionary Society
one month's missionary service   -   -   100 00
29. By Donations from Contributions in aid
of the Mission, as follows :—From a
member of Park-street church, Boston   5 00
From Mr. Wm. Kirkpatrick, Lancaster Pen. 10 00
   Mr. David I. Burr, Marietta, Ohio   5 50
   Friends at Chillicothe   -   -   6 73
   First Pres. Cong. at Cincinnati   20 00
   Female Charitable Soc. at Cincinnati   20 00
   Col. Chambers, Lawrenceburgh, Ind.
    Ter. in making change   -   1 00
Contribution at Kaskaskias   -   -   28 72
Subscription at St. Louis   -   -   -   26 50
Contribution at St. Genevieve   -   -   10 00
Contribution at Associate Reformed Con-
gregation, Springfield, Illinois Ter. -   2 18
From a lady at Vincennes   -   -   2 00
Contributions at Frankfort   -   -   -   17 50
 Do. Pres. Cong. Lexington   -   60 00
Donation from Dr. Fishback   -   -   5 00

                    220 13

Amount carried over $1530 13

Amount brought up $1530 13

June 29.   Subscription at Louisville collected
by the Rev. J. Todd.

R. Steele	-	20 00
Fetter & Hughes	-	10 00
C. & F. Bullitt	-	10 00
Thomas Prather	-	10 00
Other gentlemen	-	50 00

         100 00

Cong. and Pres. Society of South Carolina
   for promoting the interests of religion   50 00
Charitable and pious in Charleston, S. C.   40 00
Mr. C. Paulding, New Orleans   -   -   7 00
Mr. M'Mullin for preaching in the sixth
   Presbyterian church, Philadelphia   -   5 00

         202 00

June 29.   Amount of receipts to this date $1732 13
From which deduct $10 noted above as
   received from Mr. Evarts   -   -   10 00
Loss on a piece of gold received at
   Kaskaskias   -   -   -   -   90

         10 90

Amount of receipts corrected $1721 23

FINIS.

REPORT TO THE SECRETARY OF THE SOCIETY
FOR
PROPAGATING THE GOSPEL AMONG THE INDIANS
AND OTHERS IN NORTH AMERICA
RESPECTING THE INDIANS,
INHABITING THE WESTERN PARTS
OF
THE UNITED STATES
[1814]

John F. Schermerhorn

Boston 1846

REPORT RESPECTING THE INDIANS, INHABITING THE WESTERN PARTS OF THE UNITED STATES.

Communicated by Mr. JOHN F. SCHERMERHORN *to the Secretary of the Society for propagating the Gospel among the Indians and Others in North America.*

[The Society for propagating the Gospel, taking into consideration that the Indian tribes in New England are almost extinct, and that at no distant period it may be expedient to extend some portion of the income of the fund, appropriated to Indians, to tribes in the remote parts of North America, commissioned Messrs. Samuel J. Mills and John F. Schermerhorn, in 1812, to procure exact information of the state of such remote tribes, with particular reference to future missions, whenever they may be judged practicable and expedient. The following Report was communicated to the Society at their annual meeting, 26 May, 1814, and referred to their Select Committee, who authorized the publication of it in the Historical Collections. It is gratefully received, and readily inserted, as an important document in the aboriginal history of our country. EDIT.]

REV. SIR,

BY your communication of May 28, 1812, it appears, that Samuel J. Mills and myself were appointed by your Society, to obtain some information concerning those tribes of Indians, which reside west of the Alleghany mountains and the Mississippi river ; and to endeavour particularly to obtain answers to the following inquiries :

1. What is the name of the tribe ? its origin and history ?

2. What its local situation, and the extent of the territory which it occupies ?

3. What its numbers and language ? How extensively is its language understood ?

4. Whether it is independent ? or,

5. Whether in any degree dependent on the government of the United States, or any particular state? or connected with or subject to any other tribe or tribes of Indians?

6. What grants of money, goods, or other aids it receives, either from the national or any state government?

7. Whether the gospel has ever been propagated among them? If so, when? By whom? and with what success?

8. Is there any church in the nation? If so,

9. Of what religious denomination? When, and by whom established, and what its present numbers and state?

10. Is there any school in the nation? If so, when and by whom established, and what is its character and state?

11. Are they in peculiar need of religious instruction, or of schools?

12. Are they favourably disposed to receive either? and in what way can they best be supplied?

Much confusion has been introduced on part of the subject of the first inquiry, and many erroneous impressions left, from causes which, in themselves, are trifling. I mean in giving names to the different tribes.

La Hontan, Du Pratt and Charlevoix, Carver, Loskeil and others, describe many of the same tribes, concerning which they write, by different names. It was formerly a very common practice with the traders to give fictitious names to the different tribes, in order that they might not be suspected of any evil views and intentions by the Indians, were they to converse in their presence concerning their tribes. Thus it has sometimes happened, that writers have been deceived, taking the proper name of the tribe, and the fictitious name of the trader, to designate different tribes, and have accordingly described them as such. These things would lead us to suppose, that the former and present number of Indian tribes were much greater than they are in reality. In describing the tribes, I will designate them by the names by which they are known and described by the agents of the general government. The origin and history of the different tribes, except those things which relate to affairs since we have taken possession of the country, are involved in uncertain tradition and fable.

The tribes are all independent of each other, though in general they are in alliance, and occasionally meet to concert measures for their general good; as was the case in October, 1812, when there was a general council of Creeks, Chactaws, Cherokees and Chickesaws. They are, however, not independent of the United States; although we have guaranteed to them their territorial claims, still they are not at liberty to dispose of their lands, but to the United States. In short, they are considered minors; we, as their guardians.

I have not been able to procure all the information that is desirable, concerning many of the Indian tribes. I expected to have been able to present you with much important information concerning the tribes which dwell and wander in Ohio, and the Indiana and Illinoi territories. For this purpose, I wrote to Capt. Hendrick, a Stockbridge Indian of intelligence and hopeful piety, who has for some time resided among the Delawares on the White River, (I. T.) Expecting, on my return, Capt. Hendrick's particular information of these tribes, I was less particular in my inquiries concerning them, while in Ohio and Indiana territory, than I otherwise should have been. I shall, however, lay before you such information as I possess.*

WYANDOTS.

The Wyandots are a part of the Huron nation, which reside in the British dominions, on Lake Huron. Their language bears an affinity to that of the Six Nations, many of whom, particularly the Senecas, reside with them. With this tribe reside also many of the Delawares, Munsees, and Shawnees. The country they claim is in the north-west part of the Ohio, and their principal place of residence on the upper and lower Sandusky. Their num-

* Before the arrival of Mr. Schermerhorn, with the papers forming this Report, Mr. Mills returned from the mission, and, in a letter to the Secretary, observed: "We could not ascertain satisfactorily, the situation of any tribe north of the Ohio, on account of the disturbances occasioned by the war. The Indians in this portion of our western country, are generally engaged in the war against the States; and before the termination of it may, at least the greater part of them, go west of the Mississippi river." EDIT.

ber of warriors was estimated by Benjamin Hawkins, at the treaty of Granville in 1795, at 300. The probable number of souls is about 1000.

The synod of Pittsburgh have had a mission among this nation for some years, and have met with considerable success. There have been several hopeful converts to christianity, and many of the young children have been instructed in reading and writing, in which they made good proficiency. The storm of war drove them from their peaceable habitation, and they have sought refuge among the white inhabitants. They arrived at Zanestown, near Urbana, in November, 1812. They sided with us in the war. The Moravians have also had a mission among this nation. What is its present state, I cannot say. The synod of Pittsburgh feel encouraged to proceed in their mission, but are in want of funds; any assistance from any society would be gratefully accepted.

The United States have had several treaties with this nation, by which it was stipulated, in 1795, that the United States should pay to them $1000 in merchandise, as a perpetual annuity. In 1806 it was further agreed to pay them, as a perpetual annuity, $1000 in cash. In 1808, the United States gave them a gratuity of $1666⅔ in merchandise, and stipulated to pay the further sum of $400, as a perpetual annuity. This tribe receives annually from the United States $1000 in merchandise, and $1400 in cash.

SHAWNOES.

THIS tribe originally, from the best accounts I can obtain, had its residence east of the Alleghany mountains in Georgia, on Savannah river. Afterwards, part of them removed to Lancaster county, Pennsylvania and some settled in the Creek nation, and are now incorporated with them and speak the Sooanogee language. This tribe has been at war with almost all the Indians. The Six Nations and Cherokees have been their most powerful foes, by whom they have been driven across the Ohio. Since they have been north of the Ohio, they have had several places of residence on the Sciota, the Wabash, and at present, those that remain east of the Mississippi, reside near and on the Auglaize river, and on the Wabash, about Tippacanoe, (Indiana Ter.) Half of this tribe, at least, reside on the St. Francis river, (Louisiana.)

This tribe has always been reputed the most brave and skilful warriors among the Indians. The prophet, who enticed the Indians to take up the hatchet in this war against us, and his brother Tecumseh, are said to be of this tribe; though others affirm, that they are Algonquines. The language of this tribe is said to bear an affinity to the Delaware. The territorial limits between the Shawnoes, Wyandots, Delawares, Miamis, Eel river, Weas, Putawatamies, Ottoways, Pinkeshaws and Kickapoos, are, in fact, not settled among themselves, and cannot therefore be accurately defined. It is for this reason, probably, that the United States, in their purchases of lands in the Ohio and Indiana territory, have held mutual treaties with those Indians, in order to gain their general consent to the sale, and so prevent future difficulties. Strictly speaking, the Delawares and Shawnoes have no right to the lands in this part of the country. They have been permitted to dwell here by the Miamis and Wyandots, who are the real owners of the soil. This nation has been greatly reduced. Their present numbers are, perhaps 500 warriors, and 1600 souls. Half of them reside in Louisiana. By the treaty of Granville in 1795, the United States settled on them a perpetual annuity of $1000 in merchandise.

PUTAWATAMIES.

Of this nation I can say but little. They reside on the river St. Joseph, near fort St. Joseph, about the lower parts of lake Michigan. Their language is said to bear an affinity to the Chippeway, and Barton found some resemblance between them and the Indians of Darien. Their number of warriors, at the treaty of Granville, was estimated at 350; the probable number of souls 1200. They have received from the United States, since 1795, $1000 in merchandise, which is a perpetual annuity. From 1806, they receive $500 for 10 years annually. From 1808, a perpetual annuity of $400, and also at this time, a gratuity of $1666, 33. From 1810, a perpetual annuity of $500 more. So that they receive from the United States a perpetual annuity of $1000 in merchandise, and $900 in cash, besides the limited annuity and gratuities.

DELAWARES.

These reside on White river, a branch of the Wabash, in Indiana territory. They are the remnant of the old Delaware confederacy, which consisted of five tribes: the Chikohocki, Wanami, Munsey, Wabinga and Mahiccon, or Mohegan. They formerly resided on the sea coast from Delaware bay to Connecticut river. Some few families of the Mohegan still reside in Connecticut : some in New-Stockbridge, (N. Y.) but the body of the nation in Indiana territory, where the Wyandots, as early as 1751, and the Miamis since, have given them a tract of land to live on, but will not acknowledge that the Delawares have a right to sell it. The Delawares have, for several years, requested the Mohegans of New-Stockbridge, to come and settle with them ; and in that case would consent to receive a missionary among them. Many of the Stockbridge Indians have been to view the country ; some are there now, and in all probability, ere long all will remove there. This would prove a great blessing to the Delawares, for their brethren, the Stockbridge Indians, have made great progress in agriculture and civilization ; besides having a church formed among them, and at least thirty professors of religion.

The language of the Delawares must be considered as an original language ; at least, it bears no affinity to the Iroquois or Mohawk, nor to the Algonquine or Chippeway language.—See a very excellent dissertation on the Mohegan language, a branch of the Delaware nation, by Jonathan Edwards, D. D. Dr. Barton, however, is of opinion, that there is an affinity between the Delaware and Chippeway languages. The number of warriors in the Indiana territory has been estimated at 300 in 1795 ; the probable number of souls, 1000. Some of this nation have settled west of the Mississippi, on the St. Francis. The United States, in 1795, engaged to give them a perpetual annuity of $1000 in merchandise ; from 1805,

$ 600 annually for 15 years, and a gratuity at this time of
$ 1200. In 1810, they further stipulated to pay them in
cash $ 500, as a perpetual annuity. So that they are to
receive yearly forever $ 1000 in merchandise, and $ 500
in cash.

MIAMIES. WEAS. EEL RIVER.

These were originally one nation. They have the
same language and the same territory in common. Charlevoix observes, that the Miamies and Illinoi Indians are
of the same stock. From the earliest accounts we have,
they have resided on the Miamie rivers and on the Wabash. La Hontan remarks, that their language bears an
affinity to the Algonquine; Dr. Barton says, to the Delaware; Charlevoix, to the Illonese. Which of these, if
any, is correct, I am not able to say. The society of
Friends, at Baltimore, have been engaged for some time
past to introduce agriculture among them. They have
in a measure succeeded, and many of them now raise considerable quantities of corn. The agent for Indian affairs in that part of the country spoke very flatteringly
before this war, of the prospect of the Indians turning
their attention to agriculture and civilization, and adopting the manner of life among the whites.

The number of warriors among these tribes does not
exceed 500; the probable number of souls, 2000. The
population of the Miamies is as great as both the others.

The Miamies receive from the United States since
1795, $1000 in merchandise, as a perpetual annuity.
By the treaty of 1806, they received a gratuity of $400,
and a perpetual annuity of $600 in cash; by that of 1810,
a gratuity of $1500, and a perpetual annuity of $700
more. So that their perpetual annuity is $1000 in mer-
chandise, and $1300 in cash.

The Weas receive, since the treaty of Granville in
1795, $500 in merchandise, as a perpetual annuity; by
the treaty of 1806, $250 in cash, as a perpetual annuity;
and by that of 1810, a gratuity of $1500, and a perpetual
annuity of $400 in cash.

Eel River, it was stipulated in 1795, should receive
$500 in merchandise, as a perpetual annuity; in 1806,

$250 in cash, a perpetual annuity, and in 1810, $350 perpetual. Their perpetual annuity is $500 in merchandise, and $600 in cash.

KICKAPOOS

Reside towards the head of Illinoi river, and about lake Michigan. This tribe is supposed to be a part of the Shawnoese tribe. Their language, La Hontan says, is Algonquine. Their number of warriors, as estimated at the treaty of Granville, was 300 ; the probable number of souls, 1000. They receive from the United States, by the treaty of 1795, $500 in merchandise, as a perpetual annuity. By that of 1810, there was settled on them a perpetual annuity of $500 in cash, accompanied with a gratuity of $1500. Their perpetual annuity is $500 in merchandise, and $500 in cash.

PINKESHAWS

Reside near fort Outinon. They have disposed of a great part of their territory, which formerly extended from the Ohio both sides of the Wabash, some distance above Vincennes, and near to the Illinoi. Their number of warriors in 1795, was estimated at 250 ; probable number of souls 800. It was stipulated by the treaty of Granville, that they should receive, as a perpetual annuity, $500 in merchandise. In 1805, they received a gratuity of $700, and were to receive $200 annually for 10 years. In 1807, they received a gratuity of $1100, and the United States agreed to pay them, as a perpetual annuity, $300 in cash. Their perpetual annuity is $500 in merchandise, and $300 in cash.

Kaskaskias, Piorias, Cohakias and Illonese are nearly all destroyed by the Sacs and Foxes, for killing in cool blood and in time of peace, the Sac's chief, Pontiac. Those few that remain of the Kaskaskias, reside near Kaskaskia, and are very much *adulterated with French blood.* There are a few families of the Piorias, that reside on the Illinoi river, near the lake ; the other are a few wandering families. The whole number of souls does not probably exceed 500. The Kaskaskias receive from the United States, by the treaty of Granville, $500, as a perpetual annuity. In 1803, the United States stipulated to give them $500 in cash annually, forever. They also gave them, as a gratuity, at this time, $480; appropriated $300 to building them a chapel, and to pay $100 annually, towards the support of a Catholick priest.

SAUKS, OR SACS.

These principally reside in four villages. "The 1. at the head of the rapid Des Moines, on the west shore of Missisippi. 2. On the priarie, 60 miles above, on the east side of the Missisippi river. 3. On the river De Roche, about 3 miles from its entrance. 4. On the river Jowa." PIKE. They are a very warlike nation, but are more to be dreaded for deceit and stratagem, than courage. Their language, general Pike considers peculiar to themselves, and original. I am apprehensive, however, that on close investigation, it would be found that the nations in the Illinois territory have a near affinity to each other. The number of warriors in this tribe is 700; probable number of souls 2850. They receive from the United States, from 1803, a perpetual annuity of $300. They and the Foxes, who are in the closest league and may be considered as one nation, received, at the same time, a gratuity of $2234, 50.

Foxes, Reynards, or *Ottagaumeis.* The Foxes reside in three villages: 1. On the west of the Missisippi river, 6 miles above the rapids Des Moines. 2. Twelve miles in the rear of the lead mines. 3. On Turkey river, half a league from the entrance. This tribe, as also the Sacs, attend considerably to agriculture, and raise, particularly, great quantities of corn, beans, pumpkins and melons. This tribe and the Sauks are in a close league, offensive and defensive. Their language is similar to that of the Sauks. Their numbers—warriors 400; souls 1750. Their annuity from the United States, $400 perpetual.

WINEBAGOES, OR PUANTS.

In the opinion of Carver and Pike, this nation, within a century and a half, has emigrated from the west side of the Missisippi to this part of the country. Their language is that of the Otto's on the river Platte of the Missouri. They reside on the rivers Ouscousing, De Roche, Fox, and on Green Bay, in 7 villages. 1. At the entrance of Green Bay. 2. The end of the same. 3. Wuckan on Fox river. 4. At Little Puckway. 5. Portage of the Ouscousing. 6 and 7. On Roche river. They are reported brave ; but their bravery resembles more the ferocity of the tyger than the resolution of a man. A neighbouring chief drew their character thus: " A white man should never lie down without precaution in their villages." They generally speak, as do all the neighbouring nations, the Chippeway language. Their numbers are — warriors 450 ; souls 1950.

MENOMENE, OR FOLS-AVOINES.

This tribe in all probability has also emigrated from the west side of the Missisippi, as its language differs entirely from that of the neighbouring nations. The Chippeway language, however, is perfectly understood by them, and all their publick business is done in it. Their own language is said to be very difficult to acquire. They reside in 7 villages about Green Bay and Fox river. 1. At Menome river, north of Lake Michigan, and 15 miles from Fox river. 2. On Green Bay. 3. At Little Shakalin. 4. Portage of Shakalin. 5. Stenkingon, Winebago Lake. 6. On a small lake of Fox river. 7. Behind the bank of the dead. This tribe is respected by their neighbours for their bravery and independent spirit, and esteemed the peculiar friends of the whites. Their territory is not properly defined. Their hunting grounds are the same as the Winebagoes, on the Ouscousing, Roche, and Fox rivers, and on Green Bay, &c. Their numbers — warriors 300 ; souls 1350.

ALGONQUINS, OR CHIPPEWAYS.

This nation is divided into several clans or tribes. When the French first arrived in Canada, they were found on the banks and gulf of St. Lawrence to Montreal, and on the coast of Labrador. They extended also up the Ottawas river to its source. We now find them extending between the Straits of Detroit and Michigan lake ;

on the south borders of lake Superiour; the heads of the
Missisippi, Red river and lake Winipie; up the Dauphine river and Sashashawin to Fort George; from thence
with the course of Beaver river to Elk river, and with it
to its discharge into the lake of the hills; from this,
east to the isle *a la Crosse*, and by the Missisippi to
Churchill. All this must be considered the country of
the Algonquins, except a portion about Hudson's straits,
which is claimed by the Esquimaux. This nation was
formerly very numerous and powerful, but are now greatly reduced by their eternal wars, the small pox, and
excessive fondness for spirituous liquors. While the
French retained possession of Canada, they were continually fomenting wars between them and the Iroquoise.
The upper tribes have also been engaged in a war of extermination with the Sioux nation, from time immemorial. General Pike, in 1805, while on his way to the heads
of the Missisippi, succeeded in persuading them to bury
the hatchet, and plant the tree of peace. This nation is
divided into different clans or tribes, which wander
through a vast extent of territory. They do not attend
to the cultivation of the earth, but make great use of wild
rice, which grows in abundance on the lakes and fens.
Their language is copious highly sonorous, and easily ac-
quired. "It is understood by all the tribes from the gulf
of St. Lawrence, excepting the Sioux, to lake Winipie."
PIKE. They are divided into several villages or clans.

1. On an island in Leach Lake, formed by the Missisippi, containing warriors 150; souls 1100.

2. *Crees* residing on the heads of the Missisippi,
around Red lake. Warriors 200; souls 800.

3. *Musconogees*, on Red river of lake Winipie, and
mouth of Dauphine river. Warriors 100; souls 350.

4. *The Iroquoise Chippeways*, in the lake of the
Two Hills, near the mouth of the Ottawas river. War-
riors 500; souls 2000. M'KENZIE. These have two
Catholick priests among them, and are at least *christened
Indians*.

5. *Ottaways*, East side of lake Michigan. They receive from the United States, as a perpetual annuity,
$1000 in merchandise, and $800 in cash. They also re-

ceived a gratuity in 1808, of $3333, 33. Their number of warriors 300; of souls 1200.

6. *Chippeways.* East of Huron lake, in Michigan territory. They receive from the United States a perpetual annuity of $1000 in merchandise, and $800 in cash. Their numbers, perhaps, warriors 300; souls 1200.

7. *Algonquines,* residing about Rainy lake and river, and lake of the Woods. Numbers are, warriors 100; souls 300.

8. *Fols-avoin-Sauters* reside on the waters of St. Croix and Chippeway rivers. Numbers, 104 warriors; 420 souls.

9. *Knistenaux.* These are also part of the Chippeway nation, and speak the Algonquine language. They have, however, for some time, been separated from the parent stock, and in alliance with the Assinboin, a revolted branch of the Saoux. They reside on the Assinboin river and the Sashashawine. According to M'Kenzie and Pike, their warriors are 500; souls 2500. According to Breckenridge, only 300 warriors. It was my design to mention the tribes according to the natural divisions of the country; but many being so nearly allied in language, I thought it advisable to notice those which speak the same language next each other.

The following tribes reside east of the Missisippi, and north of the Ohio, to the lakes.

Tribes.	Warriors.	Souls.	Gratuities.	Perpetual Annuities. merchan.	cash.
Wyandots	300	1000	$33,666⅔	$1,000	$1400
Chippeways	300	1000		1,000	800
Ottaways	300	1000	3,333⅓	1,000	800
Shawnoes	200	600		1,000	
Putawatamies	350	1200	6,666⅔	1,000	900
Delawares	300	1000	21,000	1,000	500
Miamies	250	1000	5,500	1,000	1,300
Eel River	175	500		500	600
Weas	175	500	1,500	500	650
Kickapoos	300	1000	1,500	500	500
Pinkeshaws	250	800	3,800	500	800

Kaskaskias, &c.	150	500		80	500	500
Sauks	700	2850				600
Foxes	400	1750	} 2234,50			400
Winebagoes	450	1950				
Menomene	300	1350				
Sauters, or Fols-						
avoines	104	420				
Crees	200	800				
	5,204	19,220			$9,500	$9,750

CHEROKEES.

This tribe formerly resided on the Atlantick coast, near Charleston, (S. C.) According to tradition they drove off some tribe which possessed their present territory. They still claim a great portion of the mountainous part of Tennessee towards the south-east, and some part of Georgia contiguous to it. Their situation is high and healthy, and portions of their land very fertile. They have made greater progress in civilization and agriculture, than any Indian tribe within the United States. Many have large fine farms, and raise large quantities of corn and other grain; also flocks and herds, and make their own clothing. Many also, I am sorry to add, have a number of slaves! Their language bears no affinity to that of either of the neighbouring tribes. Loskiel observes, that it is a mixture of Shawnoese and Iroquoise. And Barton thinks it bears an affinity to the language of the six nations. They receive from the United States by the treaty of 1794, $500 in merchandise. In 1798, they received a gratuity of $5000, and $100 more in merchandise, as a perpetual annuity. In 1806, $2000 for four years, and to Black-Fox, a chief, $100 annually, and gratuity of $2000. The number in this nation, as taken by Rev. G. Blackburn, is 12,395 souls; probably 3000 warriors. There was a mission established in this tribe by Rev. Gideon Blackburn, in 1804. His attention was more particularly directed to the rising generation. He gave the rudiments of a common English education to 400 or 500 children, and instructed

2*

them at the same time in the principles of the christian religion.   There was some hopeful converts ; one among the scholars.   He was necessitated to forsake the mission for want of support.   When he came to settle the affairs of the mission he found himself $500 out of pocket ; and has since been obliged to sell his farm at Marysville, chiefly to pay this debt, and those which were necessarily incurred, while engaged in the mission, through the neglect which his private concerns suffered.   This sum has never been refunded to him.   If missionaries are left to go to this warfare at their own charges, the field will soon be forsaken.   Mr. Blackburn left the mission in 1810.   Since that time the General Assembly of the Presbyterian church have continued a school in the nation.   One of the half breed, formerly a pupil of Mr. B. has also had a school.   A Moravian has been in the nation for several years ; what has been his success I know not.   But while Mr. B. had his school in operation, and as many scholars as he could accommodate, the Moravian had not more than two or three that attended him.

The plan Mr. B. pursued was to clothe and board the scholars, and furnish the school with books at the expense of the mission.   As soon as a scholar arrived, the Indian dress was laid aside, and he was clothed after the American mode.   The children were never suffered to address an instructer, but in the English language.   Nothing was done by compulsion ; but by disgracing them for bad conduct, and rewarding merit and good behaviour. Their amusements were those of children among ourselves ; at all times endeavouring to introduce something which might be useful.   The school was opened and closed by prayer, and singing, and reading the scriptures. The progress made by the children will be seen by an extract of a history of one of the schools, containing near fifty scholars, and some letters accompanying this report. Mr. B. distributed some hundred bibles, catechisms and tracts among the children, as rewards, &c.

Here is a door opened for the spread of the gospel.   It is the opinion of Mr. B. had he been supported in the mission, that, ere this, he might have been able to extend

the mission to the Chickesaws and Chactaws, if not also
to the Creeks.

CHICKESAWS.

This tribe still claim the lands between the Missisippi, Ohio, and Tennessee rivers, to the mouth of Duck
river—up Duck river to nearly opposite Lick Creek—
from thence to the head of the North branch of Buffaloe
river, thence in a line nearly S. S. E. unto the mouth
of India Creek of the Tennessee—down the Tennessee
river to the bottom of Muscle shoals, from thence in a
straight line to where the 12° west longitude from Philadelphia intersects the 33°, 30' north latitude, and with
this parallel of latitude to the Missisippi. The States of
South Carolina and Georgia have formerly sold all their
lands, as also part of the Cherokees'; the United States,
however, since these sales, have granted to the tribes
their respective territories by treaty.

The Chickesaws were once a very powerful nation, and
their name was a terrour to all the surrounding tribes:
they carried their wars even to Mexico and New Spain,
and looked upon all the tribes on the Mobile, &c. as their
brethren. They are not now what they once were; for
although they have adopted the Yazoos, Coroas, Chiachi-
Oumas, Oufi-Ougulas, and Tapowsas, still they are but
a handful; and "to them it has literally happened, that he
that taketh the sword shall perish by the sword." Du
PRATZ.

This nation was formerly from the west of the Missisippi, at which time their warriors were estimated at
10,000. Their language, according to Du Pratz, was
once spoken by all, or nearly all, the nations in the lower
Louisiana, and appears to have been the court language
of those regions.

The New-York Missionary Society have had a mission
here for a few years; but meeting with little success, it
has been discontinued. Mr. Blackburn informed me, that
Colbert, one of the chiefs, observed, " that he perceived
the missionary was not qualified for the station, and therefore dismissed him." They are by no means unfriendly

to missions, for Mr. B. has been applied to by one of the
chiefs to open a school among them ; and that they are
sincere in this is evident from the fact, that the Indians
do support a school at their own expense. The teacher
is a vagabond ; but has agreed not to get drunk, except
on Saturdays and Sundays. I am also persuaded, that the
agent, Mr. Robertson, would favour the object. It is also a
very fortunate circumstance, that the publick interpreter
is a serious man, and hopefully pious ; as I was informed
by Mr. Bullen, the former missionary among them.
This tribe has made great progress in civilization and
agriculture. In general they are removing out of their
old villages, and clearing up small plantations, on which
they raise corn and other kinds of grain, potatoes, melons,
and cotton. The women spin, weave, and knit, and have
very comfortable dwellings. Many of them have large
herds of cattle and droves of swine, which live, winter
and summer, in the woods, without much attention.
Those who live on the publick roads sell great quantities
of corn, and sometimes prepare a comfortable meal for a
hungry traveller.—A number of the Chickesaws have removed west of the Missisippi. The number of souls in
this nation is 3500 ; and 1000 warriors. They receive
from the United States, by the treaty of 1802, a gratuity
of $700, and $3000 as a perpetual annuity ; in 1807,
they received a gratuity of $20000. G. Colbert and O.
Koy, $1000 each ; and the king $100 annually.

CHACTAWS

Reside south of the Chickesaws, and claim the country
from the Missisippi to the dividing ridge between the
waters of the Tombigby and Coose rivers, and extending
south to a little below the 32° of north latitude. From
the mouth of Yazou they sold the land for perhaps 30
miles back. They have two traditions among them of
their origin : one, that they came from the west, the
other, that they sprung out of a large Indian mound on
Pearl river. Du Pratz observes, that they were said to
have sprung out of the ground by the neighbouring
tribes, in allusion to their sudden appearance in the coun-

try, not knowing from whence they came. An old Indian gave a very rational explication of the tradition, that they sprung out of the mound between the forks of Pearl river. The banks of these streams are a marsh, and at that time probably formed an impassable ravine. There is an embankment, which served as a fortification from one branch to the other, and which, with the ravines, encloses an area of nearly three miles. He observed to the agent, S. Dinsmore, " that their ancestors, when they arrived in this country, knew not what the inhabitants were; for their own protection, therefore, they cast up this mound, and enclosed and fortified this area, to plant their corn, and as a defence against enemies. This mound served as a place for look-out, to give notice of the approach of invaders. When this was accomplished, they sent our their hunters to see what were the inhabitants of the land. These on their return reported, that they could dwell in safety, that the land was good, and game in abundance. On this they left their encampment as it may be called, and settled in different parts of the country. From this arose the tradition that they sprung or crept out of the mound." They undoubtedly came from the west. Their language is the same as the Chickesaws, with a trifling variation in the pronunciation. The Chickesaws pronounce their words short and emphatick. The Chactaws lengthen out their syllables with something of a musical cadence. These two tribes can understand each other better, perhaps, than we can a Scotchman when he speaks English. This nation is making great improvements in agriculture and civilization; the chiefs encourage it; and myself have seen, in one of their houses, spinning, weaving, and knitting; and themselves clothed in cloth of their own manufacture. They raise great quantities of corn; and also considerable stocks of cattle. and horses, hogs, poultry, &c.

The number of this nation was formerly very great. Du Pratz mentions, that they had 25000 warriors. At present they are about 15000 souls, probably 4000 warriors. It is calculated, that between 2 and 3000 of this nation have already emigrated west of the Missisippi;

and it is the opinion of their agent, that, if the United States would encourage it, they might all be removed in a few years without difficulty.

They have received from the United States, in 1802, a gratuity of $2000 ; in 1808, a gratuity of $48000 ; John Pitchlyn, $2500 ; and each of the chiefs $500. Also a perpetual annuity of $3000, and $150 to each of their chiefs, during their continuance in office.

I have had considerable conversation with the agent of this nation on the subject of missions among them. He expressed himself favourable to the object, and wished a school might be immediately opened at the agency. He assured me, that the Indians were panting for instruction, and had earnestly requested him to have schools establish- ed among them. He thinks the use of any quantity of land might be obtained toward the support of the mis- sion.

CREEKS

Is a fictitious name given to this nation by the traders, from the circumstance of the country they inhabit being intersected by Creeks. This country was formerly in- habited by many independent nations ; some of which are nearly or quite extinct ; and those that remain are con- federated and known by the name of Creeks. The Muscogees, or Middle Creeks, were intruders here, and drove off the Seminoless, or Lower Creeks ; and finally so far subdued them, as to compel them to peace and a union. So also with many other nations, which now constitute this confederacy. That the Creeks are a con- federacy of different nations, is evident from the different languages that are spoken among them. I was informed by the interpreter, who accompanied the king of the Tauchebatchee district to Fort St. Stephens, and whom I met there in April last, on my return from New Or- leans, that there were the following languages spoken in the nation at different towns—the Muscogee, Ouchee, Savanogee, Alabama, Naches, Hitchetee, Tuskegee, Oukehaee, and Queseda. Half of the nation nearly speak the Muscogee language. This nation resides south of the Cherokee. The boundary between them is the high tower; from thence west to the boundary line between the Chactaws and Chickesaws. On the west they are bounded by Mobile Bay, Alabama river, and the dividing ridge of the waters of the Coose and Tombigby. Their east and south boundary I am not able to describe. They extend, however, some distance into East Florida.

This nation have made considerable improvements in agriculture and civilization. Their conduct towards the Americans has generally been marked with deceit and insolence; and we have had more difficulty to restrain them than any other nation. They have frequently committed murders and depredations in time of peace. They are now at open war; and, were it necessary, I could trace this to its origin; but, as this is unconnected with my object, I shall omit it.

The agent of this nation is opposed to the spread of the gospel among them. He appears to be anxious to make an experiment, what can be made of man, free from the restraints of the gospel and revelation. If he has not found, ere this, that the *child of nature*, like her *scenes*, appears most perfect and beautiful at a distance, where the fancy completes the picture, he is blind indeed. This gentleman has been amusing, for some years, two Moravians with the prospect of preaching to them, as soon as they have made sufficient attainments to understand the gospel. At present they are engaged at the agency in mechanical employments. I cannot learn, that there is even a school among them to give them instruction, and thus prepare them to understand the gospel. The numbers in this nation are probably 20000 souls; 5000 warriors. Some of this confederacy have emigrated west of the Missisippi. They received from the United States, in 1797, a gratuity of $6000, and a perpetual annuity of $1500; in 1803, a gratuity of $25000 and $1000 for 10 years, and also a perpetual annuity of $3000; in 1806, $1000 for eight years, and $10000 for ten years, thereafter, besides 2 blacksmiths, for eleven years.

The Indians in the south western parts of the United
States proper, or in the states of Tennessee, Georgia and
Missisippi territory, are the following :

Tribes.	Warriors.	Souls.	Gratuities.	Perpetual Annuities. merchan.	Perpetual Annuities. cash.
Cherokees	3000	12395	$23200	$600	$3000
Chickesaws	1000	3500	29000		3000
Chactaws	4000	15000	54000		3000
Creeks	5000	20000	231000		4800
Total,	13000	50895	$337200	$600	$13800
Total of the Tribes between the Ohio and the Lakes.	5204	19220	79487	9500	9250
Total in the U. S. west of the Alleghany mountains.	18204	70115	416687	10100	23050

Of the tribes in the United States proper, the Cherokees, Chickesaws and Chactaws appear the most favourable for the establishment of a mission with the prospect
of success. To the Cherokees, the general assembly of
the Presbyterian Church have turned their attention, and
are looking for missionaries of a proper character, to send
among them. This tribe, therefore, we will leave out of
consideration, and take a view of the others—Chickesaws
and Chactaws. These two tribes are more numerous
than the aggregate of all the tribes between the Ohio and
the lakes ; and also speak the same language. From
these circumstances solely, other things being equal, a
mission would be more desirable, and the prospect of
success greater, than among either of the small tribes in
Indiana or Illinoi. There are other reasons which induce
us to give these nations the preference. They have already made great progress in agriculture and civilization,
and are by degrees casting off the Indian habit, and adopting the modes of the whites. They are generally removing
out of their villages, giving up the hunting life, clearing
small plantations, and raising domestick animals. They
have already experienced, many of them, the blessings
which flow from this change of habits, and are anxious to
make further improvements ; and many of them feel that

this is the only way left to save themselves from extermination and ruin. It is not to be expected, that they are anxious to have preaching, for of this they little know the advantages, though Mr. Bullen informed me many of the Chickesaws gave earnest attention, and appeared much affected under preaching. It is, however, more than probable, that they are anxious to have their children educated; and it will perhaps hereafter appear, that the most effectual way to introduce christianity among the Indians is, to train and instruct the rising generations in the way they should go. From the application of the Chickesaw chief to Mr. Blackburn, and the fact that they support a school at their own expense; and from what the agent observed, it appears evident, that schools, at least, might be established among them. Another thing very worthy of consideration is, that the agents of these tribes are men of reputable character, regular habits, and, if I have been correctly informed, professors of religion; and would doubtless encourage, at least, the attempt of planting a mission among them.

For the reasons that have been given, a mission among those tribes promises more success than one among the Creeks; for their languages are different in different villages, and, above all, their agent is hostile to missions. The same reasons induce me also to fix on these tribes in preference to any in Louisiana. It would be highly desirable, in a missionary view, to find a tribe uncontaminated by the vices of the whites; and where the iniquitous trader by his treachery has never learned the Indian to deceive, or by his persuasion to get drunk; but it is in vain to attempt to find a tribe in Louisiana, that has not had intercourse with the Spanish, French, British, or American trader. It is to be observed here, that we held no conferences with the Indians of those tribes on the subject of a mission among them at some future day. The situation of our national affairs, and that of those tribes themselves, was such as rendered it inexpedient. Moreover, the inquiries you desired might be made, were many of them of such a nature, had they been made to the

Indians they would have led, at this peculiar juncture, to suspicions of some evil designs, which, perhaps, it would have been impossible to remove. Neither did we consider ourselves authorized, provided we could obtain the consent of these tribes, to stipulate, that a mission would certainly be established among them *at any future time*. It was, therefore, thought unadvisable to attempt to assemble a council of the tribes. The time, when this Society shall feel it their duty, and have ability to turn their particular attention to the Indians of the west, might be so far distant, as completely to defeat the object which it was intended to promote. The Indians are very scrupulous in expecting the performance of obligations on our part, and by delay might have supposed themselves trifled with, and neglected.*

* "Respecting the tribes, residing in the Missisippi territory principally," Mr. Mills observes : " They very much need religious instruction ; and the establishment of schools among them might, most likely would, prove very beneficial to them. Many of the Cherokees very much regretted that Mr. Blackburn could not continue with them. They were ready to appropriate a considerable tract of land to be improved for the benefit of the school. The salutary effects of the mission were apparent even to the Indians themselves. I believe that there is not at present a school among either the Cherokees, Chactaws, or Creeks. I was told there was a school among the Chickesaws, but could not learn accurately the state of it. No long time since, the Chickasaw chief, or rather one of the principal men of that nation, made application to Mr. Blackburn to take up his residence with him, and pursue his own course of education with the children in the tribe. He engaged to furnish as many scholars as he could teach, and likewise to appropriate a tract of land for the benefit of the establishment. Mr. Robertson is agent of Indian affairs with this nation. He will favour any institution, which may be introduced for the benefit of the natives. Mr. Meigs is the agent residing with the Cherokees ; he is also disposed to favour the religious instruction of the Indians. He was always ready to assist Mr. Blackburn. Mr. Dinsmore is agent for the Chactaws. He is decidedly in favour of the establishment of schools among the natives, but would not so readily favour a missionary at the present time, unless he came in the character of a school master. He thinks the missionary should be acquainted with the language of the tribe he instructs, as but little confidence can be placed in interpreters. He was inclined to think that the Indians of that tribe would grant the use of as large a tract of land, as could be improved for the benefit of a school, should one be introduced among them. This tribe, as well as the other tribes in the Missisippi territory, are making considerable advances towards civilization. The Chactaw women made in the course of the last year 18 or 20,000 yards of cloth. No attempt has ever been made to introduce schools, or to give religious instruction to those belonging to this tribe. The present agent for the Creeks, if report be true, would not favour any institution among these Indians, of a religious kind. The present season cannot be deemed a favourable one for the commencement of schools, or for sending religious teachers among these Indians Their minds are much agitated by the present unhappy state of our national affairs. Some of them are evidently hostile to the United States."—*Letter to Secretary.*

WEST OF THE MISSISIPPI.

The country west of the Missisippi has been explored chiefly by Lewis and Clark, who went to the Pacifick, by the Missouri and Columbia rivers; by General Pike, who ascended the Missisippi, the Ossage, and went to the head waters of the Arkensaw and Rio Del Norte, and returned by the way of St. Fee-Antonio to Natchitoches; by Dr. Silby, who ascended the Red river, and visited the adjacent country. What I shall note concerning the Indians, west of the Missisippi, is chiefly taken from manuscripts furnished by Mr. Breckenridge, judge of the district Point-Coupee, who has himself ascended the Missouri to the Mandane villages, and visited several other parts of Louisiana, and who also had access to the manuscripts of Lewis and Clark and Dr. Silby. I shall, at the same time, compare this information with that furnished by General Pike. The few observations concerning the Indians, south of the Arkensaw river, are taken chiefly from Silby; those on Rio Del-Norte, and in New Mexico, and between the Arkensaw, the Platte and Missouri, and the heads of Missisippi, from Pike; those on the Missouri above the Platte, and to the west and north, from Breckenridge, Lewis and Clark, and M'Kenzie. Many of the tribes south of the Arkensaw are nearly extinct. Of those that remain, the chief that I shall attempt, is merely to give their names, numbers, and, if possible, their language.

CADDOQUES

Formerly resided on Red river, about 400 miles above Natchitoches; at present they reside 20 miles west of the main branch of Red river, and only 120 miles by land, west of Natchitoches. The French formerly had a settlement here. They have a tradition among them, it is said, of a deluge. The number of warriors, according to Breckenridge, is 100; souls 400. But according to another account, that I have seen, they are 3 or 400 warriors. Their language has no known affinity to any other already mentioned; but it is spoken by several neighbouring tribes.

YATTASIES

Reside 50 miles above Natchitoches, on Bagan-Piere. The French formerly had a settlement and factory at this place. These people observe, the French *were* the people the Americans *are now*. This tribe live in a fixed village, and do not exceed 100 souls; 30 men. They speak Caddo language.

NANDA-QUEES

Reside on the Sabine, 60 miles from Natchitoches. Their numbers, men 40; souls 200. Language Caddo.

ADDAISE

Reside 40 miles from Natchitoches, below the Yatta-sies. Numbers, 20 men; 100 souls. Their language differs from all others, and is extremely difficult to acquire. They speak Caddo.

ALECHE OR EGEISH

Live near Nagadoches, but are nearly extinct. The small pox a few years since committed great ravages among them. Their language, as far as it is known, is peculiar to the tribe; but the Caddo language is spoken and understood by them. Their numbers do not exceed 40 or 50 souls; 15 men.

KEYES

Reside on the Trinity river, near where the road from Antonio to Natchitoches crosses it. They are about 60 men; 200 souls, and have a language peculiar to themselves, but speak Caddo.

TACHIES

Live on a branch of the Sabine. Their language is Caddo, and their numbers 80 men; souls 300. This tribe give their name to the province of Texas.

NABADACHIES

Live in the same neighbourhood, S. W. of Sabine river. Their numbers 80 men; 300 souls.

BEDDIES

Reside on the Trinity river, about 60 miles south of Nacogdoches. They have 100 men ; 320 souls. Speak Caddo, but have a different language.

ACCO-KESAWS

Reside 200 miles S. W. of Nacogdoches, on the west side of the Colorado, and wander towards the bay. This tribe has only 80 men ; 250 souls. Their language is original, says Breckenridge. It would, perhaps, be safer to say concerning those remnants of tribes, whose language we do not understand, that we are ignorant to what language theirs bears an affinity.

MAYES

Reside on the bay of St. Bernard, near the Gaudaloupe river. They speak the Attacapas, but have a different language. Their numbers are 200 men ; 680 souls.

CORAN-CANAS

Live on an island or peninsula in the bay of St. Bernard. Their numbers are 500 men ; 1800 souls ; at war with the Spaniards. Language original ; but speak the Attacapas.

CANCES

Are a very numerous nation, and are divided into several clans or tribes, which are spread over different parts of the country, from the bay of St. Bernard to Vera-Cruz. Numbers, perhaps, 2,000 warriors ; 7,500 souls. Speak an original language.

TAN-KA-WAYS, OR TANKARDS,

Are a tribe that border on Red river, towards St. Fee. Breckenridge estimates their numbers at 200 warriors ; 700 souls. Pike says they have 600 warriors ; if so, 2000 souls.

TA-WAK-ENOES, OR THREE CONES,

Usually reside on the west side of the braces, 200 miles west of Nagadoches towards St. Fee. They are

estimated at 350 men, and 1000 souls. Their language
is said to be the same as that of the Panis or Pawnee,
on the Platte of the Missouri.

TOWEACHES, OR PANIS,

Live south of Red river, 800 miles above Natchitoches
by water, but 340 by land.   Their warriors are estimated
at 400; souls 1300.   They speak the last mentioned
language.

OPPELOUSAS

Are a few stragglers and vagabonds that wander over the
district by this name.   Their numbers 40 men; 160 souls.

ATTAKAPAS

Are also a few wandering wretches, in the district of
country to which they have given their name.   By inter-
mixture with some Tunicas, they amount to 80 men—
250 souls.

The Natchitoches, Kumas, Avogall, and Washas tribes
are extinct, or nearly so, as such; but many have united
with other tribes.

The following 10 tribes are emigrants from the Creeks
and Chactaws.

BOLUXAS

Are emigrants from Pensacola.   They came with a
few French families, and are settled about 40 miles below Natchitoches.   Their numbers are estimated at 25
men; 100 souls.

APPALACHES

Are also emigrants from West Florida, and reside on
Bayon rapid of Red river; speak Mobilian.   Numbers
15 men; 50 souls.

ALIBAMAS

Have emigrated from Florida; reside partly in Oppelousas, and some near the Caddoques.   Men 70; souls
250; speak Mobilian.

CANCHATTAS

Are of the same people with the Alibamas, and emigrated only 10 or 12 years since.   Numbers—warriors
200; souls 600; live on the Sabine.

PACANAS

Are a small tribe that reside on the Quelqueshoe river, which heads S. W. of Nachitoches. Numbers 30 men ; 100 souls; speak Mobilian, though possessing an original language.

TUNSCAS

Reside at Avogall ; are from Florida; speak Mobilian, though they have a distinct language. Warriors 25 ; souls 80.

PASCAGAULAS

Live in a small village 60 miles above Natchitoches. They are emigrants from the east of the Missisippi. It is said, they have a peculiar language, but speak Mobilian. 25 men ; 100 souls.

TENSAS

Reside on Bagou Beauf, and were formerly from Tensa river, near Mobile bay. Men 25 ; souls 100.

CHAETOOS

Live on Bagou Beauf, towards Oppelousas. They have 30 men ; 100 souls. They possess an original language, but speak Mobilian.

CHACTAWS

Are in little repute, either among white or red people. They are scattered almost over every part of Louisiana. The disrepute of this clan may easily be accounted for. They are composed of the discontented, querelous and insolent of the Chactaw nation, east of the Missisippi, who have crossed into Louisiana for the purpose of plunder, war, and to escape punishment for crimes committed in their own nation ; and some, also, because the means of subsistence by hunting were more easily obtained there, than in Missisippi Territory. Numbers, 500 warriors ; 2500 souls ; scattered over different parts of lower Louisiana.

The last ten tribes mentioned as distinct, and many of which, Silby observes, have a distinct language, though

they speak the Mobilian, have all emigrated from Missisippi territory and Georgia, and are or were parts of the
Chactaws, or Creek Indians. What Silby observes, therefore, as to their possessing a language distinct from the
Mobilian, I apprehend is erroneous ; for it is a fact that
the Chactaws and Chickesaws speak the same language ;
and Du Pratz observes, that the Chickesaws and Alibamans speak the same language. But the Alibamans, says
Dr. Silby, speak the Mobilian ; of course, to those parts
of the nation that have crossed over the Missisippi, the
Mobilian is their former tongue, and not a different language, as Silby observes.

Having found Silby so inaccurate in this plain case, I
doubt of his correctness in attributing to many tribes,
which speak the Caddo, a different language, and one
peculiar to themselves, and which has no affinity to any
other known.

ARKENSAS, OR OZARK,

Reside in three villages on the Arkensas river, not far
above the post, which is 50 miles from the Missisippi.
Those of this nation, that I have seen, are the most stupid and filthy of all the Indians with whom I am acquainted. The Chactaws are constantly making war upon them,
and at one time they were nearly extinct. At present
several of the Indians east of the Missisippi, have settled
with them, and their numbers may now be estimated at
200 warriors, and 600 souls. Their language bears a
near affinity to the Ossage.

KYAWAYS

Are a nation residing in New Mexico ; but are erratic,
and wander near the sources of the Arkensas and Platte.
They, with the Utahs and Tetaus, or Cumeehes, have a
common language. Pike estimates their number of warriors at 1000, probably 3500 souls. This nation has
immense droves of horses, and are continually at war with
the Tetaus, and sometimes with the Spaniards, Pawnees,
and Sioux.   PIKE.

UTAHS

Wander on the sources of the Rio Del Norte. They are rather more civilized than the Kyaways, arising from their intercourse with the Spaniards. They, as also the nation last mentioned, are armed with bows, arrows, and lancets. Warriors 2000; souls 7000. PIKE.

TETAUS, OR CUMEEHES, OR PADOUCAS,

Are an erratic tribe, and wander towards New Mexico, or Red river and La Platte. They are treated with great civility by the Spaniards, since they have found them a most dangerous and destructive enemy. Their numbers are estimated by Pike at 2700 warriors; 8000 souls. This nation, the Utahs, and Kyaways speak the same language.

NAMAKAUS

Are also erratic, and wander to the N. W. of St. Fee. They are frequently at war with the Spaniards. This nation is supposed to have 2000 warriors, 6500 souls. Their language is the same as that of the Appache and Le Panis, or Pawnee, and is spoken by those nations west of them, to California. PIKE.

APPECHES

Are a nation extending from the black mountains in New Mexico, to Coquillee, and keep the frontiers of these provinces in constant alarm, and render it necessary for the Spanish government to employ 2000 dragoons to protect the villages, and escort the caravans. This nation extended formerly from the entrance of the Rio Grande to California, and have carried on a continual warfare with the Spaniards, ever since they penetrated into the internal provinces. Many very heroic feats are related by Pike concerning them. Their numbers are not estimated by Pike. We cannot, from what is said of them, suppose them less than 2500 warriors, and 8500 souls.

The following table exhibits the different tribes between the Arkensaw and Rio Del Norte, which, as far as I can learn, is sometimes called the Rio Grande. The Cances and Kyaways, however, extend somewhat to the south and west of the Rio Del Norte.

Tribes.	Warriors.	Souls.	Tribes.	Warriors.	Souls.
Cadoques	100	400	Attacapas	80	250
Yattasies	30	100	Boluxas	25	100
Nan-da-quees	40	200	Appalaches	15	50
Addaise	20	100	Alibamans	70	250
Aleche	15	50	Canchattas	200	600
Keyes	60	200	Pacanas	30	100
Tachics	80	300	Tunscas	25	80
Nabadachies	80	300	Pascagulas	25	100
Beddies	100	320	Tensas	25	100
Accokesaws	80	250	Chaetoos	30	100
Mayes	200	680	*Chactaws	500	2500
Coran-canas	500	1800	Arkensas	200	600
Cances	2000	7500	†Kyaways	1000	3500
Tankards	200	700	Utahs	2000	7000
Tawakenoes	350	1000	Namakaus	2000	6500
Toweaches	400	1300	Apeches	2500	8500
Oppelousas	40	160	Tetaus	2700	8200

Total in Lower Louisiana,   15720   53890

THE TRIBES SOUTH OF THE MISSOURI AND PLATTE RIVERS, AND NORTH OF THE ARKENSAS.

OSSAGE.

This nation is divided into several tribes; the Kensas, Arkensas, Ottoos, Missouris, Mahas, Poncas, Joways, and Winebagoes. I suppose all these different tribes, strictly speaking, originally constituted but one nation, for their language, manners, and customs, are

* The number of Chactaws here noted are scattered in different parts of Louisiana, to the north, as well as south of the Arkensaw river.

† The five last tribes reside chiefly in the Spanish dominions, as now claimed by them. Our claim, however, under the title of Louisiana, extends south to the Rio De Grande Because I considered them, strictly speaking, in Louisiana, I have noted them in this place. I shall take no particular notice of the Indians in New-Spain, because I have no means of information, which can be relied on as correct. As far as I can learn, the Catholicks have missionaries among all the tribes or nations in that country.

very similar. Which of the languages of these tribes may be considered as original, and which dialectical, I am not able to determine. My reason for placing the Ossage first, and calling theirs original is, that they are first in numbers, and in character.

The Ossage tribe is divided into three clans—The Great Ossage, Little Ossage and Big Track; and may, perhaps a century hence, should they survive, be considered different nations, with as much propriety as many of the tribes enumerated. The Great Ossage village is situated on the river Ossage, 200 miles from its confluence with the Missouri. The Little Ossage, which separated from the main tribe, about 100 years since, for a long time lived on the Missouri; but not being able to withstand their powerful enemies, the Sioux, they were compelled to settle in the neighbourhood of the Great Ossages. Since peace has been established by the United States between those Indians, many of them have again returned to the banks of the Missouri. The Big Track is a party which were led off by a French trader about 20 years since, and are settled on Verdigrise river, 60 miles from its junction with the Arkensas. Great numbers join this band annually from the other bodies of the tribe; and ere long, it is probable, they will all remove to the plains of the Arkensas, on account of the superiour advantages for hunting and subsistence. The Ossage Indians have ceded to the United States all the lands between the Missisippi, Arkensaw and Missouri rivers, and a line drawn directly south from Fort Ossage, 36 miles below the mouth of Kansas river to the Arkensas. For this land they received from the United States, in 1810, the great Ossage, a gratuity of $800, and a perpetual annuity of $1000 in cash; Little Ossage, a gratuity of $400, and an annuity of $500 perpetual. The language spoken by this nation, is considered as original, at least it bears no affinity to any of the languages east of the Missisippi, except the Winebagoes, which are supposed to be descended from the same stock. Their numbers according to Pike, are,

Great Ossage	502 warriors ;	1695 souls.
Little Ossage	250	824
Big Track	500	1500
	1252	4019

According to Breckenridge, Ossages, 1500 warriors, 7000 souls.

KANSAS

Reside on the north branch of the Kansas river, 100 miles from its junction with the Missouri. The language, manners, and customs of this people, with the exception of a few local peculiarities, are the same as the Ossages. A few years since they were the greatest scoundrels on the Missouri, robbing traders, and ill treating the whites; but within a few years, in consequence of a severe defeat by the Pawnees, in which they lost their greatest and best warriors, they have been humbled, and are more peaceable. They are a stout, hardy, daring race of men, and esteemed the bravest warriors. Their numbers, according to Pike, are, warriors 465 ; souls 1560—to Breckenridge, warriors 300, souls 1300.

OTTOOS

Are supposed to be the descendants of the ancient Missouris. They speak one language, which is lofty and sonorous, and bears a near affinity in the Ossage. They reside 45 miles up the Platte from the Missouri. They are not numerous, but estimated brave. Warriors 150 ; souls 500.

MISSOURIS

Are the remnant of one of the most numerous tribes in those parts, and have given their name to the river. They have been destroyed by war and the small pox. It is supposed that none of the nations on the Missouri, or in the interior, are one half, and many of them not one tenth so numerous, as they were 25 years since. This tribe formerly resided at the mouth of the Grande river.

At present they reside and are incorporated with the Ottoos.   Warriors 50 ; souls 300.

MAHAS

Reside on the Missouri, principally at Mahas Creek, 240 miles above Platte river.   They are very friendly to the whites, and have considerable trade.   Their manners, customs, and language, are similar to the Ossage.   They have been greatly reduced, as to numbers, within 10 years. Their present numbers are 250 warriors ; 800 souls.

Mr. Breckenridge related to me, that the principal chief, or king of this tribe, was a very wicked and cruel man ; that he pretended to have familiar intercourse with spirits ; and would frequently foretell the death of some of his people.   The events so regularly happened, according to his predictions, that immediately on his telling a person that he should die, the man began his death song, and died accordingly.   It was supposed, that before the king made such declarations, he took some means to administer to them some subtile poison.   This produced great fear of him, among the Indians ; and after his death they took his body, placed it in a sitting position, on his finest horse, and raised a large mound over them, and now worship him, as the Indians do the evil spirits, to appease their wrath, and avert their anger.   Will this circumstance of of the *mound* afford a clue to the probable design of some *mounds found in the western country ?*

PANIS, OR PAWNEES,

Are a tribe from New Mexico, and formerly was a part of the famous and implacable enemies of the Spaniards, the Appeches.   There are two other branches of this nation, which have been already noticed, the Ta-wak-enoes, and Toweachas on Red river.   The Pawnees are divided into three clans.   The Pawnee proper, Republicans, and Loups.

The Pawnee proper are said to have made considerable progress in civilization, and generally treat traders and whites, who visit them, with respect and hospitality. They reside on the south side of the Platte, about 100 miles from its mouth ; the Republicans, on the Republican branch of the Platte; the Loups, on Wolf river. This tribe has no idea of the exclusive right of soil; they claim only what they possess. They hunt on the Platte and Kensas. Their language, I shall denominate the Appechee, because I consider them sprung from that stock, and because there is a near affinity between the two languages. Their numbers, according to Pike, are,

Pawnee proper	1000	warriors;	3120 souls.
Republicans and Loups	485		1485
	1485		4605

According to Breckenridge,

Pawnee proper	400	warriors;	1600 souls.
Republicans	350		1400
Loups	300		1400
	1050		4400

ARICARIES

Are also a branch of the Appeches, as is evident from the affinity of their language, and similarity of their customs, to the Pawnee. They must also have emigrated from New Mexico. They reside now on the Missouri, in two villages, about 1440 miles from the Missisippi. This nation is said to be very industrious, and frequently to have corn three years old. They are very dissolute in their manners, as will appear hereafter. Formerly they were very numerous, as is evident from the number of deserted villages; their numbers are estimated at 250 warriors; 800 souls. This tribe, like the Pawnee, have no idea of exclusive right of soil.

PONCAS, OR PONCARS,

Formerly were a very numerous tribe; but at the beginning of this century were driven from their habitations, and nearly extirpated by the Sioux. During their war with the Sioux, and until 1811, they led a wandering life. They now reside on the Missouri, a few miles below the Quiacre river, 1000 miles from the Missisippi. Their character is that of thievish, marauding, insolent, and vicious. Their language is the same as the Mahas, and they are probably descended from the same stock, Ossage. 50 warriors ; 300 souls.

MANDANS

Reside about 1600 miles up the Missouri, in two villages, a few miles below Knife river. Formerly, this tribe was numerous, and, according to their traditions, consisted of 17 villages; which is rendered probable, from meeting in this part of the country, with the ruins of many deserted villages. This goes to corroborate what has been in another place advanced, that many of the tribes on the Missouri, have been reduced to half, others to a tenth, of their former population. The language of this tribe, is not known to have an affinity to any other ; they, however, speak the language of the Gross-ventres. 350 warriors ; 1250 souls. At these villages was erected a fort and trading establishment in 1811.

A-WA-HA-WAS, OR SAULIERS.

This is a small tribe, which reside only three miles above the Mandan villages, on the Missouri. According to their tradition, they originally constituted a part of the Crow-Indians, but in consequence of a quarrel of two chiefs, over the carcase of a buffaloe, which both claimed, a separation took place. They speak the Crow language ; live in one village. 50 men ; 300 souls.

Minetares, or Gross-ventres, Fall, or Big-bellied, or Paunche Indians. These are different names given by different persons to the same nation ; as they are divided in different bands, and live in different parts of the country. Minetares, or Gross-ventres, reside in four villages, on both sides of Knife river, near its confluence with the Missouri, five miles above the Mandan villages. Breckenridge is of opinion, that these, as well as the Sauliers, formerly constituted a part of the Crow nation ; though they have been in their present villages, as far back as their traditions extend. They speak the same language as the tribe last mentioned. If *they* speak the Crow language, these speak the same. Warriors 600 ; souls 2500.

FALL, OR BIG-BELLIED INDIANS,

Sometimes called *Gross-ventres* of the *Priarie*, reside at the confluence of the north and south branches of the Saskatshawine river, and extend from thence to the great bend in the Missouri, in latitude 47° 30′ north. Numbers, according to Breckenridge, 500 warriors, 2000 souls. M'Kenzie, 700 men. "Speak the Crow language."
                                                        BRECKENRIDGE.

PAUNCHE, OR AL-LA-KA-WE-AH,

Live on the Yellow Stone river, and wander in different parts, on the heads of the Missouri, near the Rocky Mountains. This tribe is said to be hospitable and peaceful. Numbers, 800 warriors ; 2500 souls. Supposed to speak the Crow language.

CROW-INDIANS, OR ABSAROKA,

Are divided into four bands, and wander on the Yellow Stone, and Bighome rivers on the heads of the Missouri, and Rache-jaune, and even to the west of the Rocky Mountains for 200 miles, where a party of them was met by Mr. Robert Steaurt of New York, in 1812, on his return from the Pacifick ocean. The different bands of this nation are very numerous, and estimated at 900 warriors, and 3500 souls. Whether the language of this nation bears any affinity to any of those west of the Rocky Mountains, I am not able to say, and therefore note it as a language peculiar to themselves ; and consider the Gross-ventres, Fall, and Paunche Indians, and Sauliers, as being originally of the same nation, and having with them a common language.

CHYENNES.

This tribe wander on the heads of Chyennes and White rivers. Breckenridge observes, that they speak a language peculiar to themselves, and are of a remarkably fair complexion. It is said this is the tribe, that has been supposed to be Welch Indians, whose progenitors emigrated to this country under Madoc ; and to whose work, by some, are attributed the Indian *mounds* in the western country. It has been confidently asserted, in proof of the existence of a tribe of Welch Indians, that parts of a Welch Bible have been found among them, and that a Welchman, who visited them, conversed with them in their own language. Granting it to be a fact, which we very much doubt, that this supposed Welch tribe have parts of the Welch Bible among them, we can safely affirm, that it was not received from the adventurers under Madoc; for he left his country some centuries before there was an edition of the Welch Bible printed. That a Welchman has conversed with a tribe of Indians in the Welch language is, to say the least, extremely improbable; when we recollect the change which language undergoes in pronunciation, within half a century, among nations which have a written language, how much greater must be the diversity in pronunciation, produced between two clans of the same tribe, that have been separated for upwards of six centuries; and that, too, when the separating clan has no written language to guard it from changing its original pronunciation? But, admitting that they have retained it, is it probable, that a Welchman of the 19th century, could converse intelligibly with one of the 12th century, were it possible to produce such an one? It may be shown from history, that Madoc sailed with a colony from Wales; but that he planted them in America is an assumption without sufficient proof. It can be proved, only from the existence of such a tribe. The principal arguments to prove this fact have been considered. What weight they ought to have, to substantiate this fact, is for the reader to judge. The arguments drawn from the complexion and beard of the supposed Welch tribe, cannot weigh much, when it is considered that the same appearances are common among other tribes. One nation being more cleanly, and living in a different latitude, will, at least in part, account for fairer complexions; and the practice of eradicating the beard, is by no means universal among the American Indians. We hazard nothing in saying, that the existence of a tribe of Welch Indians in America, is ideal, and nothing but a hoax of some trader or traveller, played on the credulous.—To return from this digression.

4*

The Chyennes, it is said, formerly resided on or near Red river of lake Winipie, and were driven from thence to where they now live, by the Sioux. Carver mentions the Schians as a band of the Sioux. Can this be the same tribe as we now call the Chyenne ? This tribe with the Stactan, Kata, Nemausin and Dolame, four small tribes, which also live on the heads of Chyenne river, are estimated at 500 warriors ; 2000 souls. I know not to what nation, or nations, the four bands just mentioned belong, nor what language they speak ; the probability is, they belong to the Chyenne, and are only different bands of the same tribe.

WATEPAHATOES.

This tribe reside on the Paducas fork of Platte river, but are not stationary. I presume they are a band of the Kyaways already mentioned, and with whom frequently they reside. If so, they speak the same language as the Utahs and Tetaus. 200 warriors ; 900 souls.

KENENAVISH.

This tribe is erratic, and lives on the heads of the Yellow Stone river. I have not been able to ascertain to what tribe they have an affinity. Their numbers are estimated at 1500 warriors ; 5000 souls.

PASTANOWNAS, OR CASTAHANAS.

This people are also erratic, and live between the sources of Padoucas fork of Platte and the Yellow Stone rivers. 400 warriors ; 1500 souls.

SNAKE-INDIANS.

This nation is divided into three principal tribes, which are again subdivided into several bands or clans. They are a peaceable and defenceless people, and are frequently killed and enslaved by their neighbours. They wander from the falls and sources of the Missouri, on the heads of the Yellow Stone, Platte, and Arkensaw to Red river and New Mexico. They are supposed to be, at least, 1000 warriors ; 5000 souls. Breckenridge observes, they speak a language peculiar to themselves.

INDIANS BETWEEN THE ARKENSAW AND MISSOURI RIVERS.

Tribes.	Warriors.	Souls.	Tribes.	Warriors.	Souls.
*Different tribes from east of Missisippi.	700	3000	Awahawas	50	300
			Gross-ventres	600	2500
Ossage	1252	4019	Crow	900	3500
Kansas	465	1565	Chyennes	500	2000
Ottoos	150	500	Watepahatoes	200	900
Missouris	50	300	Kenenavish	1500	5000
Mahas	250	800	Pastanownas	400	1500
Pawnee	1485	4605	Snake	1000	5000
Aricaries	250	800			
Poncas	50	300	Total	10152	37839
Mandans	350	1250			

TRIBES NORTH OF THE MISSOURI AND WEST OF THE MISSISIPPI.

JOWAYS.

This tribe reside in two villages, one on the Joway, the other on the Des Moyens river. They were originally a part of the Missouri tribe, from whom they separated, and have since conquered them, and now claim their country by right of conquest. They speak the Ossage language. They, the Sauks and Reynards, have sold all their right to the land east of the Missisippi, between the Jafflone and Joway rivers, as far as the Missouri. Warriors 300; souls 1400.

SIOUX, OR NAUDUWASSIES.

This is a numerous, warlike, and brave people. Their language bears no affinity to any of the neighbouring nations, and is very guttural. In this, perhaps, it differs from the language of most Indians, many of which are highly sonorous, sweet, and lofty. Barton thinks this nation is a branch of the Wyandot. This is not probable; for the Wyandot itself is a branch of the Huron, which was originally a part of the Iroquois; as is evident

---

* These are composed of the Shawnoes, Wyandots, Delawares, Cherokees and Chickesaws.

from the similarity between their languages. This nation is divided into several tribes ; these again subdivided into different clans. The subdivisions I shall not particularly note. The principal tribes are, 1. Minoway-Kantong, or Gens De Lai. 2. Washpetong, or Gens De Fieulles. 3. Saussetons. 4. Yanktons. 5. Titons. 6. Washpecoate. 7. Assinboin.

MINOWAY-KAUTONG

Reside on the Missisippi, from the Prairie De Chiers to Prairie De Francois, 35 miles up the St. Peter's. They are reported the bravest of all the Sioux tribes ; and are the only one that attend to agriculture, and that in a very small degree. Their country is well timbered and watered. Men 305 ; souls 2105.—PIKE.

WASHPETONG

Reside on the N. W. side of the St. Peter's, to the mouth of Chippeway river.—BRECKENRIDGE. At Prairie Des Francois, near the Roache Blanche, on the St. Peter's.—PIKE. Their numbers are estimated, by Pike, at 1060.

SAUSSETONS

Reside on the upper parts of Red river, of lake Winipie and the St. Peter's, and rove on the Missisippi and Corbeau rivers, which is the boundary between them and the Chippeways. They usually meet the Titons and Yanktons in May, with whom they trade. Men 360 ; souls 2160.—PIKE.

YANKTONS

Have a fixed habitation. They are divided into the Yanktons of the north and the south. Those of the north wander on the heads of St. Peter's and Red river of lake Winipie, and trade on the Missisippi at St. Peter's. Those of the south are settled from Montague's Priarie to the rivers Des Moyen and Missouri, and trade at Jacque river. The country over which they wander, in parts of it is pleasant, well timbered and watered. Warriors 900 ; souls 4300.—PIKE.

Titons

Reside on both sides of the Missouri. On the west side, from near Chyenne river to the Mandan villages, and on the N. E. from the Mahas villages to near the Gross-ventres, or Knife river. They are not permanently fixed; and like the wandering Arab, their hands are against every man. They are the pirates and marauders of the Missouri. They, as also the Yanktons, have the finest horses, and travel with incredible celerity, being in one place to day, and 500 miles distant ten days hence. Warriors 2000; souls 11600.—Pike.

Washpecoate

Rove on the S. W. of the St. Peter's, from a place called *Hard Wood* to the Yellow Medicine river, and hunt on the heads of the Des Moyen. This was formerly a part of the Washpotang tribe, and is composed of the outcasts of all the other tribes. Men 900; souls 4050.—Pike.

These six tribes of the Sioux claim the lands west of the Missisippi, beginning at the Joway river above the Prairie Des Chien to the St. Peter's; thence on both sides of the Missisippi to Corbeau, or Crow-wing river, up the same, including its waters, to the head of Red river; thence westerly, bearing south, so as to intersect the Missouri, at or near the Mandan villages. Here their line crosses the Missouri, so as to include the lower parts of the Chyenne river, the whole of the waters of the White and Teton rivers, and the lower parts of the Quicure; from thence easterly, bearing north, to the place of beginning. These tribes have waged a war of extermination with the Chippeways from time immemorial, and almost destroyed many of the tribes on the Missouri, and east of the Missisippi. They have also waged a long war with the Assinboin, one of the tribes that separated itself from the nation. The numbers of these bands are, according to Pike, 3835 warriors; 21675 souls.
—— to an Officer, 2590   7610
—— Breckenridge, 2000   6000
       Probably 2500 warriors, 10000 souls.

ASSINBOIN

Are a revolted band of the Sioux, with whom they have long been at war. Like the parent stock, they are divided into different bands, and reside in different parts.

THE OSEGAH

Reside about the mouth of little Missouri, and on the Assinboin, at the mouth of Lapelle river. Warriors 25 ;* souls 850.   [* Probably 250. EDIT.]

MANITOPA

Live on the Saskatshawine, or Mouse river. Warriors 200 ; souls 750.

MAHTOPANATS

Wander on the Missouri, above White-earth river, and on the heads of Mouse, or Assinboin river. Warriors 450 ; souls 1600. The whole number of Assinboins ; 900 warriors ; 3000 souls.

BLACK FEET.

This nation is erratic, and wander on the heads of the Saskatshawine and Missouri rivers, and on the Moria river, and along the Rocky ridge, or mountains. They are divided into different tribes ; Black feet, Blood-Indians, Picaneaux, or Catanoneaux, &c. all of which, says M‘Kenzie, are a distinct people, and speak a language of their own, and which has no affinity to any language which he has heard. This nation is very hostile to the hunters and traders that attempt to ascend the Missouri, and pass to the Pacifick. Warriors 2500 ; souls 8000.

CHIPPEWYAN.

This is a very large nation, who consider the country between the parallels of latitude 60° and 65° north, and longitude 100° and 110° west, as belonging to them. They speak a very copious language, which is very difficult to acquire, and which is spoken with a slight variation of dialect by all the tribes living between Hudson's bay and Rocky mountains, and north of the Missisippi and the ridge which divides the waters running north from those which enter lake Winipie ; with the exception of the

Esquimaux who inhabit the north coast. This fact was ascertained by Mr. A. M'Kenzie, in his voyages of 1789 and 1793, who found that the Rocky Mountain Indians; Sarsees, Slave, Beaver, Dog-rib, Hare, Strong-bow, Mountain, Quarrellers, and Knife Indians; in short, all those tribes that reside on M'Kenzie's, and Peace rivers, and on the adjacent waters, spoke dialects of the Chippewyan tongue; and he also found, that the Indians on Columbia river, as low down as latitude 52°, 24′ north, and from thence to the Pacifick, spoke dialects of the same language. What the numbers are of these tribes, east of the Rocky mountains, is difficult to determine. When, however, we consider the natural situation of the country, and its very high latitude, we are ready to draw the conclusion, that the numbers are small. All the Chippewyans, that visit the different establishments of the N. W. company, do not exceed 800 men, nor probably 2500 souls. The other tribes mentioned, we are led to conclude from M'Kenzie's account, are very small; probably none of them exceed 500 souls; all of which cannot exceed 1200 men, 5000 souls; and I am not certain that many of these small tribes are not included in M'Kenzie's estimate of the Chippewyans. The whole numbers of these tribes east of the Rocky mountains, which speak the Chippewyan language, are, 2000 warriors; 7500 souls.

ESQUIMAUX.

This nation, it would appear, from similarity of language, manners, and customs, was originally from Greenland. It is the opinion of the Moravians that visit them, that there is no more difference between their language and that of Greenland, than between high and low Dutch. This people are found, with certainty, from the coast of Labrador, west to M'Kenzie's river; and have been found as far north as 72°, by Mr. Hearne, in 1772. Captain Cook further reports, that he found the same people on the islands and coast, of North America, opposite Kamskatka and at Norton's sound, Ooneleshka, at Prince William's sound. See Rees' Cyclopedia, *Esquimaux*.

M‘Kenzie is of opinion, that the people inhabiting
the coast of the Pacifick differ, both from the Chippewyans, and Esquimaux. It is not to be supposed, that
a country, covered with snow for more than half the year,
and whose summers do not exceed six or eight weeks,
can be very populous. What the numbers of this nation
are, cannot be precisely ascertained. They have been estimated at 1623 souls: the whole number, from Labrador
to M‘Kenzie's river, we should not suppose could exceed 5000 souls, 1200 warriors. The Moravians have a
missionary establishment on the coast of Labrador, at
Nain.

MOUNTAINEERS.

This people live on the interior of Labrador, and are
enemies to the Esquimaux. I know not what language
they speak, unless it is a dialect of the Algonquine.
Their numbers are small; perhaps 300 men, 1500 souls.

INDIANS WEST OF THE MISSISIPPI, AND NORTH OF THE MISSOURI AND LAKES.

* In the United States and Louisiana.

Tribes.	Warriors.	Souls.	Tribes.	Warriors.	Souls.
Joways	300	1400	Fall Indians	500	2000
Sioux	2500	10000	Paunche	800	2500
			Total	4100	15900

In the British dominions.

Tribes.	Warriors.	Souls.	Tribes.	Warriors.	Souls.
Mohawks	300	1000	Knistenaux	1500	5000
Iroquois } Chippeways }	500	2000	Assinboin	900	3000
			Black-Feet	2500	8000
Hurons	250	800	Chippewyans } & tribes of the } same language }	2000	7500
Leach-lake- } Chippeways }	150	1100			
Musconoges	100	350	Esquimaux	1200	5000
Algonquines } of Rainy lake }	100	300	Mountaineers	300	1500
			Total	9800	35550

* I suppose, in this table, the boundary line between the United States and
the British provinces to run on the ridge, which divides the waters running
into the Missisippi and Missouri from those that enter lake Winipie and the
Saskatshawine river.

I shall probably hereafter complete something more full on the Indian government, character, manners, education, religion, and morals. This I had not the leisure to do at present, and must therefore defer it for a future communication, if it shall be thought desirable by your reverend body. I may possible add to this some hints concerning a plan for conducting Indian missions. I trust that this communication, imperfect as it is, will be in some measure useful and satisfactory to your Society. With my best wishes for its prosperity and usefulness, receive the assurance of the esteem and respect of your friend and servant,

JOHN F. SCHERMERHORN.

Rev. ABIEL HOLMES, D. D.
    Sec. Soc. Prop. Gospel, &c.

[NOTE. In the MS. copy of the preceding REPORT the same Indian names are diversely written, but corrections could not be obtained from the author; a circumstance the more to be regretted, as he had not prepared the MS. for publication. EDIT.]

Religion in America
Series II

An Arno Press Collection

Adler, Felix. **Creed and Deed:** A Series of Discourses. New York, 1877.

Alexander, Archibald. **Evidences of the Authenticity, Inspiration, and Canonical Authority of the Holy Scriptures.** Philadelphia, 1836.

Allen, Joseph Henry. **Our Liberal Movement in Theology:** Chiefly as Shown in Recollections of the History of Unitarianism in New England. 3rd edition. Boston, 1892.

American Temperance Society. **Permanent Temperance Documents of the American Temperance Society.** Boston, 1835.

American Tract Society. **The American Tract Society Documents,** 1824-1925. New York, 1972.

Bacon, Leonard. **The Genesis of the New England Churches.** New York, 1874.

Bartlett, S[amuel] C. **Historical Sketches of the Missions of the American Board.** New York, 1972.

Beecher, Lyman. **Lyman Beecher and the Reform of Society:** Four Sermons, 1804-1828. New York, 1972.

[Bishop, Isabella Lucy Bird.] **The Aspects of Religion in the United States of America.** London, 1859.

Bowden, James. **The History of the Society of Friends in America.** London, 1850, 1854. Two volumes in one.

Briggs, Charles Augustus. **Inaugural Address and Defense,** 1891-1893. New York, 1972.

Colwell, Stephen. **The Position of Christianity in the United States,** in Its Relations with Our Political Institutions, and Specially with Reference to Religious Instruction in the Public Schools. Philadelphia, 1854.

Dalcho, Frederick. **An Historical Account of the Protestant Episcopal Church, in South-Carolina,** from the First Settlement of the Province, to the War of the Revolution. Charleston, 1820.

Elliott, Walter. **The Life of Father Hecker.** New York, 1891.

Gibbons, James Cardinal. **A Retrospect of Fifty Years.** Baltimore, 1916. Two volumes in one.

Hammond, L[ily] H[ardy]. **Race and the South:** Two Studies, 1914-1922. New York, 1972.

Hayden, A[mos] S. **Early History of the Disciples in the Western Reserve, Ohio;** With Biographical Sketches of the Principal Agents in their Religious Movement. Cincinnati, 1875.

Hinke, William J., editor. **Life and Letters of the Rev. John Philip Boehm:** Founder of the Reformed Church in Pennsylvania, 1683-1749. Philadelphia, 1916.

Hopkins, Samuel. **A Treatise on the Millennium.** Boston, 1793.

Kallen, Horace M. **Judaism at Bay:** Essays Toward the Adjustment of Judaism to Modernity. New York, 1932.

Kreider, Harry Julius. **Lutheranism in Colonial New York.** New York, 1942.

Loughborough, J. N. **The Great Second Advent Movement:** Its Rise and Progress. Washington, 1905.

M'Clure, David and Elijah Parish. **Memoirs of the Rev. Eleazar Wheelock, D.D.** Newburyport, 1811.

McKinney, Richard I. **Religion in Higher Education Among Negroes.** New Haven, 1945.

Mayhew, Jonathan. **Observations on the Charter and Conduct of the Society for the Propagation of the Gospel in Foreign Parts;** Designed to Shew Their Non-conformity to Each Other. Boston, 1763.

Mott, John R. **The Evangelization of the World in this Generation.** New York, 1900.

Payne, Bishop Daniel A. **Sermons and Addresses,** 1853-1891. New York, 1972.

Phillips, C[harles] H. **The History of the Colored Methodist Episcopal Church in America:** Comprising Its Organization, Subsequent Development, and Present Status. Jackson, Tenn., 1898.

Reverend Elhanan Winchester: Biography and Letters. New York, 1972.

Riggs, Stephen R. **Tah-Koo Wah-Kan; Or, the Gospel Among the Dakotas.** Boston, 1869.

Rogers, Elder John. **The Biography of Eld. Barton Warren Stone, Written by Himself:** With Additions and Reflections. Cincinnati, 1847.

Booth-Tucker, Frederick. **The Salvation Army in America:** Selected Reports, 1899-1903. New York, 1972.

Satolli, Francis Archbishop. **Loyalty to Church and State.** Baltimore, 1895.

Schaff, Philip. **Church and State in the United States** or the American Idea of Religious Liberty and its Practical Effects with Official Documents. New York and London, 1888. (Reprinted from *Papers of the American Historical Association,* Vol. II, No. 4.)

Smith, Horace Wemyss. **Life and Correspondence of the Rev. William Smith, D.D.** Philadelphia, 1879, 1880. Two volumes in one.

Spalding, M[artin] J. **Sketches of the Early Catholic Missions of Kentucky;** From Their Commencement in 1787 to the Jubilee of 1826-7. Louisville, 1844.

Steiner, Bernard C., editor. **Rev. Thomas Bray:** His Life and Selected Works Relating to Maryland. Baltimore, 1901. (Reprinted from *Maryland Historical Society Fund Publication,* No. 37.)

To Win the West: Missionary Viewpoints, 1814-1815. New York, 1972.

Wayland, Francis and H. L. Wayland. **A Memoir of the Life and Labors of Francis Wayland, D.D., LL.D.** New York, 1867. Two volumes in one.

Willard, Frances E. **Woman and Temperance:** Or, the Work and Workers of the Woman's Christian Temperance Union. Hartford, 1883.

DATE DUE

7/26/74			
GAYLORD			PRINTED IN U.S.A.